IS YOUR BED STILL THERE WHEN YOU CLOSE THE DOOR?

...AND OTHER PLAYFUL PONDERINGS

New York London Toronto Sydney Auckland

IS YOUR BED
STILL THERE
WHEN YOU
CLOSE THE DOOR?

...AND OTHER PLAYFUL
PONDERINGS

*How to Have Intelligent and Creative
Conversations with Your Kids*

JANE M. HEALY, PH.D.

PUBLISHED BY DOUBLEDAY
a division of Bantam Doubleday Dell Publishing Group, Inc.
666 Fifth Avenue, New York, New York 10103

DOUBLEDAY and the portrayal of an anchor with a dolphin
are trademarks of Doubleday,
a division of Bantam Doubleday Dell Publishing Group, Inc.

Library of Congress Cataloging-in-Publication Data

Healy, Jane M.
  Is your bed still there when you close the door? . . . and other playful
ponderings : how to have intelligent and creative conversations with your kids /
Jane M. Healy.—1st ed.
    p.   cm.
  Includes bibliographical references.
    1. Communication in the family—Miscellanea.   2. Thought and think-
ing—Miscellanea.   3. Creative ability—Miscellanea.   4. Parent and child—
Miscellanea.   5. Language development—Miscellanea.   I. Title
HQ784.Q4H4   1992
306.874—dc20   91-25251
                                                                        CIP

ISBN 0-385-41762-4
Copyright © 1992 by Jane M. Healy, Ph.D.

Other books by Jane M. Healy
YOUR CHILD'S GROWING MIND
ENDANGERED MINDS

BOOK DESIGN BY CAROL MALCOLM-RUSSO

All Rights Reserved
Printed in the United States of America
May 1992
1   3   5   7   9   10   8   6   4   2
First Edition

This book is dedicated to my mother,
whose curiosity and love of learning
still show me the way . . .

. . . and to the children of the world,
who will seek answers
to questions that haven't yet been asked.

ACKNOWLEDGMENTS

I am deeply grateful to the teachers, administrators, and students of the Vail Mountain School who invited me into their classrooms for "intelligent conversations." Their lively response enriched this book immeasurably, while the vibrancy, originality, and depth of their thinking reaffirmed my hopes for our collective future. Their frequent pleas for "more questions" were pleasant reminders of the power of this technique to "hook" young folks into expanding their creative use of higher-level thinking.

Many thanks also to Ginny Crowley, Gretchen Larson, and Mary Krogness, who commented on the selection of "Read-Alouds," and to Nancy West for her helpful suggestions on the manuscript. The constant encouragement of John Duff and Angela Miller helped immeasurably, and I am grateful to them both for their creative support of the book's possibilities. John's thoughtful editing was first-rate!

Our sons, Scott, Jeff, and Doug, and their friends enthusiastically volunteered as conversational guinea pigs, helping me select and refine the questions. One of the best by-products of writing this book was rediscovering the perspicacity and wit that make our kids some of the most interesting people we know!

And of course, as always, Tom makes it all possible.

CONTENTS

Part One
TEACHING CHILDREN TO THINK

1

Part Two
OPENING MINDS

3 1

Part One

TEACHING
CHILDREN
TO THINK

THE BOY WHO COULDN'T THINK

Having intelligent conversations with young people is easier than most adults believe, and it's one of the most dependable brain-builders around. Moreover, talking with kids can be a lot of fun! But many of us are skeptical about our ability to communicate effectively with the younger set. What is an "intelligent conversation," anyway, and how do we get one started?

Not long ago, a father of two school-aged youngsters challenged me for some practical answers to these questions. He came up and introduced himself after a lecture, somewhat ambitiously entitled "Developing Creative Minds for the Twenty-first Century," in which I had emphasized the importance of good "talk" in fostering the thinking skills necessary for our young people's future success. From the disgruntled expression on his face, however, I could tell he was not delighted with my message.

"I don't want to be difficult," he began, "and I'm sure we should talk more with our children. But the last thing my wife and I need is another guilt trip! We're both working, and our time is so limited. Don't just tell us to have 'intelligent' conversations. Tell us *how*! This isn't 1950 when everyone sat around the dinner table for hours every night. Give us some practical ideas, not just vague prescriptions!"

To my chagrin, I realized I didn't have a ready response. Everyone knows how to talk to their kids, don't they? I thought back to our sons' growing-up years. Snatches of dialogue replayed themselves in my mind:

ME: Well, how was school today?
CHILD: OK
ME: Did you learn anything interesting?
CHILD: Not really.

I guess some tips might come in handy, after all!

THE IMPORTANCE OF "TALK"

During the next few months I puzzled over how to respond to this man's challenge, which stuck to my mind like a provocative little burr. Professionals are working on effective new techniques to use when conversing with young people because they know that correctly structured "talk" can:

- enhance brain functioning of children and teens

- develop mental skills that lead to academic success

- lay the groundwork for mathematical and scientific reasoning as well as for reading and writing

- teach children to express themselves effectively

- boost SAT and other standardized test scores

- differentiate among students who will be educationally "advantaged" and those who will seem "disadvantaged"—whatever their family income or circumstances

- give children a competitive edge in an "information age"

- prepare young people for leadership positions

- reduce fighting and delinquent behavior

- develop creativity and problem-solving abilities

But what practical tools could help parents and teachers open the door to such conversation? Was there some "magic key" that would be realistic, fun, relatively easy and efficient—and still get the job done?

THE BOY WHO COULDN'T THINK

I was still wrestling with these questions when a student gave me an idea. Eleven-year-old Daren came to me for educational therapy because he had a serious "motivation" problem. Moreover, he had difficulty understanding what he read, solving math "story" problems, and thinking through ideas in science and history lessons. And yet he was bright, with an IQ well above average! I suspected Daren probably had a specific learning disability, but extensive testing failed to pin down a diagnosis. Gradually I became convinced there was a deeper problem: Daren had never learned how to think! If answers didn't immediately appear, he simply gave up.

"I really haven't the faintest idea," was his stock response to any question requiring mental effort.

Curious, I invited his mother over for an informal conference to find out what kind of thinking Daren was encouraged to do at home. A likable and obviously intelligent lady, she was genuinely worried about her son's mental lassitude.

"How can we help?" she wanted to know.

I inquired about how the family spent their time together. What kinds of things did they talk about?

"Oh, we talk when we have dinner together." She thought for a moment. "But actually, I guess my husband and I mostly talk, and the children just sit there long enough to eat and then get away to their TV programs."

As we continued to talk, I realized that Daren lived in a household where he was rarely asked or expected to take any kind of intellectual initiative. It was assumed that most issues had "right" answers, about which parents knew more than children, and conversations centered on practical everyday details of family life. With little incentive to do any independent thinking, it wasn't too surprising that Daren had trouble with mental problem-solving.

Ironically, his school compounded the problem. Repetitious worksheets, memorization of information, and multiple-choice tests and quizzes (where there was always a right answer and no room for discussion) predominated. In many classes, teachers did most of the talking and students were not encouraged to disagree, discuss issues with each other, or, in some cases, even to ask questions. Yet his teachers were the ones complaining he was mentally passive!

A WEIRD ASSIGNMENT

An an experiment, I decided to give Daren's whole family a homework assignment. Would they be willing to try a different variety of conversation at dinner—to nudge Daren and his six-year-old sister toward more creative, independent thinking?

His mom readily agreed to some simple rules for discussing a question which, like those in Part Three of this book, *didn't have any right or wrong answer.* The first one we chose was:

"How might the world be different if people were born with wheels instead of feet?"

Such "open-ended" questions have been used by corporate trainers to teach business managers how to

- think more creatively

- solve problems more effectively

- give everyone an opportunity to participate

Because there is no "right answer," adults and children as young as five or six can become involved together, and adults are often amazed at the way children "open up" in a nonjudgmental atmosphere where they know their ideas will be listened to without criticism.

I waited eagerly for my next meeting with Daren. When he arrived, I couldn't contain my curiosity. What had happened at dinner?

"Well, we talked about this weird question," he explained.

"Was it interesting?" I prodded.

"Yeah, but we all had some different ideas. Even Susie had a pretty good idea—and Dad and Mom had some, too. It was sorta fun because no one was right and no one was wrong. That was the biggest rule—you had to listen to everyone else and you couldn't tell anybody they were wrong. And you know," he added, "I never thought much about why all the things we use are built like they are—but if people had wheels instead of feet they'd have to be different! Houses, and bikes, and clothes. . . . It's sorta fun to think about."

"Would you and your family like any more 'homework' like that?" I ventured.

"Sure. Have you got any more questions?"

PARENTS AS INTELLECTUAL PLAYMATES

Although I won't claim Daren's academic future was rehabilitated by one dinner-table conversation, that episode marked an important beginning for him—and for this book, which will help you use open-ended questions to guide the young people in your life toward higher-level thinking. It will provide provocative brain food, not only at the dinner table, but in the carpool, during "downtime" in the classroom, or wherever you find minds (including grown-up ones) able to stretch and grow. I suggest you first review the next two chapters, which explain why open-ended thinking and the related conversational skills are so important. In Part Two you will find specific guidelines for using open-ended questions as well as tips on how to get and keep a conversation rolling. All these hints are inspired by the latest research and have been field-tested in homes and classrooms. Part Three contains the questions, which I call "Playful Ponderings," grouped into levels according to difficulty.

In exploring these "weird" ideas, I hope, above all, you

will have fun. Playfulness and a spirit of adventure loosen the laces and tickle the toes of creative imagination. As parents and teachers we can—and should—be intellectual playmates for our children! In the process, we show them how to expand their minds to the skills that will help them become productive thinkers and leaders in the world of the future.

WANTED: CREATIVE MINDS FOR THE FUTURE

*H*ave you ever tried to imagine what the world will be like when your children are grown? What new challenges will confront them? What skills they will need for personal success and as creative leaders in a technological world? What kind of thinking power will be most important—and how can you make sure they have it?

Educators who have searched for answers to these questions agree on one thing: Because of dramatic changes spurred by new technologies, the "basics" of tomorrow are skills we now view as "higher-level" ones. This means that a person who is not good at open-ended thinking and problem-solving—whatever his or her IQ—will soon be left behind.

If your child avoids new or startling ideas, is unable to speculate or "guess," or has difficulty thinking of multiple solutions to problems, please pay close attention to the chapters that follow. Youngsters displaying these danger signals are already on the road to intellectual passivity.

"BASICS" FOR THE TWENTY-FIRST CENTURY

Increased partnership with the computer mind is altering traditional demands on the human brain in many ways:

- The amount of available information is growing at such an accelerated rate that the human brain cannot learn even a small portion of it.

- Increasingly portable computers are replacing many of the functions of human memory. They can be used to store, categorize, and retrieve most of the bits of information, or data, that have filled school curricula and dominated homework assignments (e.g., facts, dates, names, formulas, etc.).

- Many traditional learning tasks, such as memorizing spelling words and drilling on rules for long division, will become less important as computers do them more efficiently and accurately.

- The emphasis in learning must shift from remembering information to understanding and organizing it. Human brains will not only have to comprehend and prioritize this mass of information but also make informed judgments about how to use it.

Clearly, our views of education—and thinking—are in for some alterations. While students will doubtless continue to need a good grounding in the traditional "basics" of reading, writing, and understanding arithmetic (as well as in how to fix the computer when it breaks!), our culture will demand many more "thinking skills" than ever before. Moreover, the workers of the future will need special kinds of brainpower to remain smarter than the machines!

If you want to prepare your children for these challenges, make sure they develop initiative, "big-picture" thinking, open-ended problem-solving, the ability to tolerate uncertainty, communication abilities, skills of cooperation, and, perhaps most important of all, the ability to ponder.

Initiative

Contemporary life tends to make children more mentally passive than they should be. While television and computer games have some educational benefits, electronic media generally tend to manipulate children's attention; the machines set up their own agendas and induce the viewer to follow an external lead instead of initiating ideas.

Yet the successful minds of the future will be those that have learned what it feels like to be in charge of themselves. They will be able to direct their own attention and come up with their own action plans.

Our frantic family schedules also get in the way of independent thinking as we propel children through activities designed by adults. Many children today don't have time to play with real objects or games—much less with ideas! Poor preparation for the leaders of tomorrow who must be well prepared to initiate original ideas and to believe they are worth pursuing.

Big-Picture Thinking

The wondrous talents of the human brain enable it to approach thinking in many different ways. One of the most interesting differences occurs between two major types of processing: (1) *step-by-step, detail-type thinking,* which you might use when adding a series of numbers or proofreading a manuscript, and (2) *"global," intuitive reasoning,* which helps us with such tasks as grasping the meaning of a "story" problem in mathematics, understanding the motives of a character in a novel, or imagining a design for an original invention. Obviously, both uses of the brain are important and necessary, and we constantly utilize both.[1]

Some people find it alarming that present-day computers are rapidly surpassing the human brain in the ability to do the first kind of thinking—the detail work. On the other hand, machines cannot manage the "big-picture" reasoning that combines intuition, intelligence, and practical experience for understanding—the type so important for our children to develop, and the type fostered by the activities in this book.

---

1. *For a fuller description and an explanation of how these types of thinking relate to your child's brain development and "learning style," see my first book,* Your Child's Growing Mind *(New York: Doubleday, 1989).*

14

Warning: If we neglect our children's imagination and intuition while stuffing them with details and skills that can be performed more effectively by machines, we are setting them up to become obsolete in the blink of a cybernetic eye.

Open-Ended Problem-Solving

When most of us went to school, questions had answers. In fact, they usually had *one right answer*, which we needed to know in order to pass the test on Friday. Gradually, however, the game has changed, though many schools haven't yet caught on to the new rules. Perhaps this transformation began when scientists discovered that the "facts" of Newtonian physics—which they had taught unquestioningly—might not really be true after all. Suddenly, members of the scientific and philosophical community were forced to start questioning the very basis of what they thought they "knew." (See *The Dancing Wu Li Masters* by Gary Zukhov if you would like a fascinating explanation of this mental watershed.)

Of course, no one denies that some questions still have right answers:

"Can I play in traffic?" No!

"Should we try to be kind to other people?" Yes!

"What is 8 × 7?" 56 (if you're working in base 10, at least).

But many of the questions our children will confront do not have such obvious solutions:

"Is it OK to patent a new bacterial life form that will provide a cure for cancer but might also prove to be a dangerous long-term addition to the environment?"

"Should we allow companies to clone people's bodies (with brains removed) so that each individual will have a set of duplicate organs in case of disease or damage?"

"What is the best solution to the problem of nuclear waste disposal?"

Minds capable of grappling with such issues must be able to see more than one side of a question, to adopt multiple perspectives, to generate various answers before settling on a "right" one. They will also need the personal value system and mental perspicacity to distinguish between the "givens" ("Don't play in traffic") and the "possibles."

Ability to Tolerate Uncertainty

Open-ended thinking requires something else that is difficult for those of us who were raised in "one right answer" environments: comfort with a certain degree of ambiguity or uncertainty. Our children will need the ability to suspend judgment until all possible ideas are out on the table to avoid premature closure of topics or minds. This skill is a distinguishing characteristic of creative people in all disciplines and a "must" for successful thinkers in an uncertain future. Fortunately, programs to teach "thinking skills" have shown that adults can improve their own abilities—as well as those of their children—by using some fairly simple techniques. They are incorporated into the suggestions given later in this book for the *conversation game.*

Communication Abilities

It is a sad irony that conversational skills are suffering more in this "information age" than ever before. Teachers everywhere lament the inability of their students to get ideas into words—either orally or on paper—and *listening skills* should be on the "endangered species" list! Many hard-working parents admit they have little time or energy to devote to extended conversations. Family dialogues tend to focus on the nitty-gritty of survival in a busy world:

Parent: Everyone ready? Got your books?
Child: Yup. You picking us up after school?
Parent: Nope. Take the bus today. I'll be home at six.

While such dialogues are necessary and get the immediate job done, they do little to enhance either language development or thinking skills.

Contrary to what many people believe, television is more of a culprit than a help, as it does not teach children either to listen actively or to express themselves. Computer games and even educational computer programs also tend to focus on fast-paced visual activities. No one disputes the growing importance of visual media, but success in a "global society" will also require advanced communication skills—possibly in more than one language. Our children are learning to communicate in gestures and sound bites, but if parents want them to do well in life as well as in school, conversational skills—both listening and speaking well—should be a family priority.

Skills of Cooperation

Does it seem odd to regard "cooperation" as a skill that must be learned? Educators have recently been surprised to find that it is! In fact, we have just begun to realize that our society has encouraged children to compete (for grades, for the teacher's attention, for teams, for awards, etc.) to the point where they may have difficulty doing things cooperatively. Yet employers increasingly report that one of the most important characteristics of people they want to hire is the ability to work with others to get a job done.

As the glut of information thickens, even garden-variety specialists will have to cooperate more frequently with people in allied areas of specialization. An obvious example is in the field of medicine, where it is now common practice for doctors with different specialties to collaborate on a case because no one of them can keep up with all the new developments in each area of expertise. So also in many other fields; the information explosion makes collaborative problem-solving increasingly important. Family and classroom environments, properly structured, are natural means for exposing children to the satisfactions of mutual problem-solving as well as to the boosts and bruises of competition.

The Ability to Ponder

When I ask groups of parents or teachers how long it has been since they heard the word "ponder," they laugh ruefully. We all know that we—and our children—need more opportunity to explore the quiet recesses of our own thinking, but who has the time? Yet a society that neglects its philosophers, no matter how much effort it devotes to developing technicians, is in for big, deep trouble. Knowledge cries out for the leavening power of wisdom. Our children will never learn to think reflectively unless we give them time and space to imagine, to wonder, and to push against the boundaries of ideas.

HOW THIS BOOK WILL HELP

The activities in this book incorporate each of these skills. If you take the time to try out some meaningful conversations, suspending the need for "one right answer," listening to and valuing everyone's ideas, grappling with novel questions, and trying to tie down abstract thoughts with words, you will be giving your children an automatic leg up into the next century. As we shall see in the next chapter, you may also be increasing their brain capacity.

WHOSE BRAIN IS GROWING TODAY?

"Good grief," sighed a colleague after a recent conference on "Language, Learning, and the Brain." "If I'd known all this, I sure would have taken the time to talk—and listen—more to my kids."

Many parents today are concerned about how to "stimulate" their children's brain development, but they all too often go about it in the wrong way. Lessons, "educational" television, cram courses, and many other kinds of "learning" activities may misfire if applied without a basic understanding of mental development. In fact, all the intellectual effort adults spend trying to make offspring smarter may be increasing their own brainpower more than that of the kids!

If I told you that you can do more to build your child's intelligence at your family dinner table than in all those fancy "enrichment" experiences, would you believe me? In this chapter we will briefly overview some of the reasons. To begin with, here are important guidelines gleaned from current research:

- Getting children personally interested and involved is much more effective than trying to "make" them learn something.

- Active participation—mental or physical—is essential for higher-level learning.

- Engaging children's curiosity may be the secret ingredient for brain-building.

- Proper training of the brain's language circuits underlies logical reasoning.

- Good conversational habits improve problem-solving skills and school grades and may even prevent some forms of learning disability.

- Children's everyday adult models for thinking are more important than outside instruction.

ACTIVE INVOLVEMENT BUILDS BRAINS

Cells in the brain grow stronger and heavier not only by maturation but also by being actively used. Thus, thinking and learning experiences make a significant difference in the degree to which each individual brain reaches its potential. If some abilities are rarely tapped in childhood, the neurons that serve them may fail to develop fully. For example, youngsters who do not hear—and practice using—good language (i.e., the kind that they will need to understand literature or communicate effectively in the adult world— irrespective of tongue or dialect) during preschool and elementary years may have ongoing difficulty mastering advanced verbal skills. Those who are not shown how to consider a problem thoughtfully and follow a plan for action may develop a permanent pattern of impulsive behavior. [1]

Two fundamental principles worth repeating:

1. If we want children to develop certain skills, we must see to it that they practice them.

2. The best catalysts for intellectual growth are curiosity and active participation; merely observing others learning will not do the trick.

For little children, active involvement naturally translates into physical action. For older youngsters, thinking hard about ideas, asking questions, trying to figure out ways to do things or solve problems all qualify as brain-builders.

IT'S NEVER TOO LATE!

Generally speaking, the younger the brain, the more susceptible it is to the effects of learning experiences. It is important to note, however, that connections for new and more complex types of learning continue to become available all during childhood and adolescence. Active curiosity and personal interest are such powerful forces, in fact, that even geriatric

---

1. *These ideas are explained in detail in my book* Endangered Minds *(New York: Simon & Schuster, 1990).*

brains can change and grow somewhat if these factors are present.

WHOSE BRAIN IS GROWING TODAY?

1. **Who asks most of the meaningful questions, adults or children? Questions like "When do we eat?" or "Did you do your homework?" don't count!**

The brain that is genuinely interested and searching to make sense out of its environment is likely to be the one getting the most expansion.

2. **Do you spend a great deal of effort arranging activities and lessons to make children smarter—or do you set up situations where they can follow the lead of their natural curiosity?**

Excessive efforts to organize or force learning on children may enrich your own brain instead of the "victim's."

3. **Do you allow your children (or students) to express ideas even if you don't agree with them?**

Although children certainly need *rules for behavior*, minds bound by too many *rules for thinking* may lose their curiosity. (This goes for teachers as well as for parents!)

4. **Do you show children what active learning looks like by modeling curiosity, openness, and interest in new ideas and challenges—or did your brain stop growing somewhere along the way?**

Children learn more from what we show them than from what we tell them. That's why the activities in this book are designed to get everyone's brain engaged—from six-year-olds to grandparents!

"TALK": A TOOL FOR BUILDING BRAINS

The ability to reflect on our own thinking—and talk about it—is what makes human intelligence so powerful. Moreover, the process of learning to use language to think about ideas and communicate them to others has powerful effects on brain development, although these uses of language do not always come naturally. Research shows that normal youngsters pick up language basics without half trying—they just absorb them like oxygen. The refinements, however, must be learned and practiced with the help of a supportive environment. They include:

- understanding more advanced sentence structure (the kind found in books or conversation above fourth-grade level)

- expressing ideas accurately and concisely

- comprehending and using specialized vocabulary

- expanding "social" functions of language (persuading people to cooperate or "selling" a point of view, inferring another person's motives)
- using language to plan, talk through problems, and pay attention

The very process of exercising these higher-level language circuits in the brain strengthens and expands them. Unfortunately, many children in today's video generation are being short-changed on this kind of stimulation, which may help explain the rash of learning problems in our schools. Teachers—and test results—tell us that many students now show specific weakness in these particular skills, with difficulty in paying attention leading the list.

How "Talk" Helps Kids Pay Attention
A former student of mine, Amy, was a perfect example of a youngster who didn't know how to use words to organize her thinking. Labeled "impulsive" by the school psychologist, she jumped feet first into any task—and usually ended up in trouble. When the teacher handed out an assignment, Amy would be half finished before the directions were given; naturally, her accuracy suffered.

"This child can't pay attention," wailed her teacher. "And I can't get her to slow down long enough to follow directions!"

The picture brightened, however, after we worked with Amy on a technique called "verbal mediation." She learned a four-step procedure that basically boils down to:

Stop and Think
Talk About the Problem
Talk About Your Plan
Follow Your Plan

Now Amy is able to use her quick mind more effectively because she learned to use the "control functions" of language to help manage her thinking.

Another student, Mark, dramatically improved his reading comprehension once he understood that it was important to talk to himself about what he was reading. Mark had never learned to use "inner speech," the internal dialogue that good readers use to clarify and anticipate the events and ideas in a story. Because he was not using language effectively to deal with ideas, Mark also had difficulty talking or writing about abstract concepts such as "friendship" or "heroism." When a teacher showed his parents how to help him with these powerful uses of language, however, his thinking sharpened along with his reading.

Children who learn to think through problems or ideas by talking about them do better on tests of attention and also in overall school performance. Fortunately, the "executive" control systems of the brain that are responsible for this progress can be stimulated by the type of conversations recommended in this book.

TEACHING CHILDREN TO TALK MEANS TEACHING THEM TO THINK

Children learn their language—and thinking—habits in great part from their home environments. Research shows that children from families who tend to "mediate" situations verbally—that is, talking thoughtfully about problems or questions—are better readers, writers, communicators, and reasoners than those from families using language less effectively. Conversation-rich environments also help youngsters develop the powers of inner speech, which include problem-solving, memory, and planning as well as reading comprehension. If you want your child to do well in math and science, as well as in overall thinking ability, be sure to include nourishing conversations in your daily household menu!

ANTIDOTE FOR PASSIVE CLASSROOMS

How wonderful it would be if all schools understood—and celebrated—the importance of active involvement, curiosity, and "talk" to build brains. While many do, others, unfortunately, do not. Parents may have to work hard to counteract the effects of the "average" classroom where:

- teachers talk 90 percent of the time (and students "tune out"—who can blame them?)

- 95 percent of questions are rote-level, factual ones ("In what year did such-and-such happen?" "What's the answer to problem 3?")

- students are not encouraged to express—or even think about—ideas and are prohibited from discussing what they are learning with each other

Foresighted educators are trying hard to get all students more dynamically connected to the curriculum. In the meanwhile, however, parents should not assume schools are teaching their children to talk—or to think—very effectively.

I'M SOLD: ARE YOU?

If this chapter has sounded like a sales talk, it was! I hope you're sold on *why* it's so important to make time for good conversation in your children's lives. Now it's time to get on to the *hows*.

Part Two

OPENING MINDS

~~~~~ F O U R ~~~~~

QUESTIONS WITHOUT
ANSWERS:
THE KEY TO OPENING
MINDS

*We learn more by looking for the
answer to a question and not finding
it than we do from learning the
answer itself.*

—Lloyd Alexander, author of the
Prydain Chronicles

HOW TO STOP A CONVERSATION

Despite their value in getting people thinking and talking
together, open-ended questions without any "right" or
"wrong" answers are difficult for many adults to handle. I
was forcibly reminded of this fact when some friends agreed
to let me use them and their three children as guinea pigs in
trying out questions for this book. Yes, they would be
delighted to have a family conversation while I eavesdropped.
Unfortunately, however, we failed to discuss the ground
rules. After all, I knew I was dealing with very intelligent
people. That was my first mistake!

Seated comfortably in their family room, I proposed a problem—*"What would happen if money actually began to grow on trees?"*—and waited for the interesting ideas to surface. They never did. The father, sensing a golden opportunity to educate his two offspring about a topic on which he was very well informed, launched into a monologue about the history of our monetary system. We other adults were too polite to interrupt, and the children simply ignored these gems of wisdom and wistfully eyed the television, which had been extinguished for the occasion. So much for family discussion! So much for creative thinking! So much for opening minds!

The next day, I experienced the opposite situation with a parent who helped her children expand their thinking. Amid a literal explosion of ideas, they covered topics that ranged from environmental implications (trees would be stripped and might not survive) to practical considerations (Child 1: "I would go buy everything I wanted." Child 2: "But if everyone could pick all the money they wanted, why would anyone work in the stores?") to economic and political theory (What is "money" anyway if it loses its value; would another form of currency be needed—and who would decide?).

GETTING RID OF THE "ONE RIGHT ANSWER" MENTALITY

My friend, like so many adults, had been well trained to feel uneasy if he didn't have an instant (correct) answer for any question that was asked. Indeed, the process of opening up toward the possibility of ideas rather than quickly closing down to facts and solutions was downright threatening to him. He didn't want to be caught even for a minute with his answers down—*especially in front of his children*! His reasoning process looked like this:

CONVERGENT THINKING

But the object of this book is to make a reasoning process that looks like this:

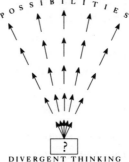

DIVERGENT THINKING

Before you read any further, please accept these two promises:

1. **No one will give you a failing grade if you can't answer these questions.**

2. **Your children will not think less of you if they discover you are not omniscient.** (Besides, guess what—they have already figured it out!)

SHOWING CHILDREN HOW TO THINK

Children tend to model their thinking habits after those of their parents and, to a lesser degree, of their teachers. If we want our children to be strong reasoners and creative thinkers, we must show them how to use their minds flexibly and take intellectual risks. It can be risky to propose a new idea or follow up on an intriguing thought that isn't in any textbook. If can also seem risky to admit you don't know the answer. Yet, when children see adults who can say, "I don't know, but that's an interesting question. . . ." or "I never thought about that before, but let me try. . . ." they learn firsthand about intellectual curiosity. While "right" and "wrong" certainly have their places, wise parents and teachers also create safe spaces for this kind of inquiry.

"BUT, I'M JUST NOT THE CREATIVE TYPE"

Because most of us are far better at convergent than divergent thinking, we may need to retool our own intellectual habits in order to provide these models. As a reformed convergent thinker, I can guarantee that it's not too late to learn even if you're absolutely sure you're not creative! Following the guidelines given here will definitely unlock mental flexibility as they lure you and your children into habits of strong, creative reasoners:

HOW DO CREATIVE THINKERS THINK?

"BRAINSTORMING"
THINKING FLUIDLY, FLEXIBLY, AND ORIGINALLY
SUSPENDING JUDGMENT
AVOIDING THE "FUNCTIONAL FIXEDNESS" TRAP

- *Brainstorming*, the first step in problem-solving, gets the creative juices flowing and lets people stimulate each others' thinking by getting as many ideas out as quickly as possible. Sometimes brainstorming leads directly to important new ideas or solutions. Other times, it simply dissolves the logjam of blocked thinking. You'll learn specific steps for this process in Chapter 7.

- *Thinking fluidly* means having many ideas; *flexibly* means being able to shift easily from one idea to another; *originally* means coming up with novel or unique thinking. These three characteristics are often used to define "creativity." They all require a climate in which children know they will be listened to and won't be criticized or ridiculed for their suggestions.

• *Suspending judgment* is essential in developing the atmosphere necessary to break through into creative problem-solving. Studies of people who have trouble solving their real-life dilemmas show they often settle too quickly on an answer or course of action, without considering enough possibilities. Good thinkers avoid getting prematurely bogged down in particulars.

• *Avoiding "functional" fixedness"* means not being stuck too firmly to habitual ideas that are no longer useful. A classic experiment published by N. R. F. Maier in 1933 illustrates the situation:

> You enter a room to find two ropes suspended from the ceiling. The experimenter asks you to tie the two ends of the ropes together and assures you it is possible. On a nearby table are a few tools, including a hammer and pliers. You grab the end of one rope and walk toward the other rope, but you can't reach the second rope. You try to extend your reach using the pliers but still cannot grasp the other rope. What do you do?

At this point, many people give up. Those who succeed in solving the problem have to think of an unconventional way to use the pliers. Can you do it?

(Hint: Tie the pliers to the end of one rope, making a pendulum of it so you can get it swinging far enough to catch hold of it while grasping the other rope.)

Most great scientific breakthroughs have come when someone envisioned a new way of looking at everyday objects or ideas. Psychologists also call this talent "breaking set." Adults who are good models of this kind of thinking purposely arrange situations where there is time and emotional space to play with alternatives, toy with "weird" suggestions, and explore novel perspectives. Incidentally, parental encouragement of this type of intellectual risk-taking correlates highly with the development of resourcefulness in children!

CHILDREN AS PHILOSOPHERS

By opening the door to thinking, we also stand to learn from our children. Gareth Matthews, a teacher and author of *Philosophy and the Young Child*, who has spent a lifetime developing methods to teach philosophy to elementary-age students, knows that children have deep and significant thoughts. Yet he has also observed that adults rarely give them enough credit for their ability to reflect on interesting and important questions. During many hours spent discussing the questions in this book with children of all ages, I have become convinced that a latent philosopher does indeed lurk beneath the skin of most youngsters. But in order to hear what the children have to say, we must *stop lecturing and start listening*. The next two chapters explain how to make this switch.

HOW TO LISTEN
TO CHILDREN

Adults skilled at listening to children have more fun as well as better relationships with the youngsters in their lives. Let me share with you a few important pointers I've picked up over the years. The key to the whole process lies in understanding that children think and reason differently from the way adults do. Their ways are not necessarily inferior—just different.

Although it seems obvious, we tend to forget that our extra years of brain development confer certain advantages. The physical maturation of neuron connections, combined with an accumulation of learning experiences, enable different tools for reasoning. Children's reasoning tends to be more *concrete*, relying heavily on firsthand, real-life experience and personal associations. Adult reasoning, on the other hand, can be more objective and *abstract*, incorporating concepts (like "democracy," or "proportion") that are not seen, felt, or experienced firsthand.

Generally speaking, the younger the children, the harder it is for them to grapple with abstract concepts. A preschool teacher recently laughed as she told me about a lesson that didn't quite work for this very reason. She had decided to teach her class of three- and four-year-olds about the concept of "air." After introducing the idea, she issued small plastic bags and dispersed the children around the classroom in search of this invisible commodity. After some tense moments, each child eventually captured some air; they squeezed the bags, heard them "whoosh," and engaged in a myriad of other activities before the lesson concluded. "Air is everywhere," the teacher emphasized for a final time. One week later, curious about how much they remembered, she brought out the plastic bags again. Off went her charges in search of air.

"I wouldn't have believed this," she chuckled later, "but every single child went back to the exact same spot where they had previously found their 'air'—and I couldn't persuade them that it might be someplace else, as well! I guess 'air' is more abstract than I realized!"

While older children and adolescents have moved up several pegs on the conceptual scale, they, too, are still immature in many understandings. Thus we shouldn't be surprised if they can't always "see" and generalize ideas as we do. In conversing with young people, rule number one is to *try to tune in to their reasoning*. Do not assume they are viewing things as you are, because they probably aren't.

KIDS AND ADULTS THINK DIFFERENTLY

Here are some talents that grown-up brains tend to exercise more readily than those of younger folks. As you try out the questions in Part Three of this book, be on the lookout for examples of these and other differences:

• *Understand another person's point of view*

This means not only empathizing with someone's feelings but also being able to understand the reasons for another's opinions or motivation if they are different from your own. One Mom I know spent a great deal of time and effort explaining to her eight-year-old daughter her personal reasons for going back to work. It soon became clear that what the child really needed to hear about was how she would be taken care of and what this would mean in terms of her own daily routines. As much as she loved her mother, her immature mind naturally centered on her own personal, here-and-now experience.

• *Get a perspective on time, space, and other abstract ideas*

If we want elementary school students to understand history, for example, we must make it meaningful for them with stories, pictures, and projects. Even then, it is not uncommon to find seven-year-olds who are a bit unclear about whether or not their great-great-great-grandparents might have met any cavemen! They aren't unintelligent; their brains simply do not have the breadth of reasoning to put such things into perspective. Likewise, children need to learn science by doing experiments, not by hearing about them. Relative distances are also hard for concrete thinkers to grasp. I know a typical child who is convinced that Cleveland is closer to Disney World in Florida than to Cincinnati because it takes longer to get to the latter (by car) than to the former (by plane). Even showing him maps can't shake his faith; lines and dots on paper are abstract; his own firsthand experience is what makes sense to him!

• *Plan ahead or anticipate consequences*

Children's difficulty envisioning what might happen or thinking into the future often puzzles and frustrates parents and teachers who find such concepts obvious. In September of the school year, two anxious parents fell into a common trap of promising their third-grader they would buy him a bike in June if he got all A's. At this age, however, it is hard to plan ahead even for one day, much less a whole year, so this kind of "motivation" is predestined to fail. Long-term assignments for "research reports" or science fair projects for elementary-age children also run afoul of these developmental realities. Unless the planning is taught as part of the whole project, parents usually end up feeling pressured to mastermind the outcome.

• *Reason logically about moral and ethical issues*

Children tend to be very personal in their views about

abstract moral principles. "When asked, 'Why do we have laws?' one seven-year-old gave a typical response for this age: "Because Charles might steal my bubble gum on the playground and it isn't fair!"

Around age ten or eleven, many youngsters become very concerned about topics of this sort and begin to generate remarkably mature ideas. Research suggests, however, that a surprising number of adults are themselves unable to do this type of "higher-order" thinking. Even older teenagers, while naturally drawn to questions about moral issues, still need lots of practice. If such reasoning is important to you, be sure you demonstrate it.

• *Understand cause and effect*

What makes things happen? How do seemingly "magical" consequences come about? Adults can analyze such situations, but although we may assume children have the same ability, they don't. One of my favorite experiences in this regard occurred when a mother came up after a workshop to ask if I thought her son should take saxophone lessons.

"He really wants to," she said.

"How old is your son?" I asked.

"Five," she replied.

Long pause . . .

"What did your son say that makes you think he wants to take sax lessons?" I finally inquired.

"Well, every day he says, 'I want to play the saxophone.' "

Don't we all! Here is a wonderful example of a miscommunication between a child, who is simply making a statement out of his own point of view ("I want to play the saxophone") and a mom hearing it with hers ("I want to take lessons"). Her adult brain understands (he doesn't) what goes into playing this instrument (many lessons, tiresome practice, etc.). This child is not asking for all that hassle; he's merely stating a childish wish.

We all, including veteran teachers, sometimes forget that even bright children speak "child," not "adult." A lower-school principal told me about an incident that confirmed this message for her. To her surprise, two of her brightest fourth-graders had confided they were afraid to go into the middle-school building next door where they were supposed to wait for their rides after school.

"But you're perfectly safe there," she admonished.

Doubtfully, the youngsters eyed each other.

"But what if no one speaks English?" one girl finally asked.

Totally baffled, my friend considered this seemingly illogical comment. In this school almost everyone spoke English almost all of the time! Then the light dawned. The corridor in the middle school through which these children passed on their way to the lunchroom housed the classrooms of the foreign language teachers. During their break, they often stood in the hall chattering happily in French and Spanish while the little ones filed by.

"I would have thought these kids were old enough to understand," she sighed, "but I guess this shows you never can be too sure!"

Teachers often tell small children, "Put on your listening ears" as a concrete signal for them to pay attention. Although I personally view this comment as somewhat patronizing when applied to children, we might well transfer it to ourselves. If you want to have intelligent conversations with children, give your own assumptions a rest, put on your listening ears, and hear what the child is really saying.

COGNITIVE LEVELS: WHAT TO EXPECT

It is dangerous to assign ages to stages of development because children vary so much, but here's a rough idea of what you can expect as you try out these "playful ponderings" with participants of different ages.

UP TO FIVE YEARS: Children are very "self-centered," believing everyone sees the world from the same perspective they do. They also have difficulty generalizing situations outside their own experience, such as understanding that what they see on television news will not necessarily happen to them or their family. They are probably too young to be included in the conversations suggested in this book, except perhaps as interested bystanders. But even three-year-olds sometimes come up with profound comments!

FIVE TO SEVEN YEARS: Children of this age group are making an important transition into more sophisticated thinking. They can begin to grasp general concepts like "friendship" or "heroism" if they have firsthand experience with them. They will be likely to respond to any question with a personal association (e.g., Question: "What would the world be like if we had no way of keeping time?" Response from Suzie, age six: "My grandma gave me a watch for my birthday.") While such associative responses are typical of this age, children in this interesting transition period may sometimes contribute substantially to a discussion. Most five- and six-year-olds will probably fluctuate between the role of a spectator and that of a participant in the conversations suggested here. As they listen, their own thinking will be stretched.

AGES SEVEN TO ELEVEN (OR TEN, OR TWELVE, OR . . .): In this period, which theorist Jean Piaget termed "concrete operations," children gradually become more able to reason about ideas—although it still helps to tie them down to familiarity. Don't be surprised if youngsters at the beginning of this age period still think quite rigidly and are intensely concerned with judgments of good/bad, right/

wrong, fair/unfair. Most nine-, ten-, and eleven-year-olds can reason more broadly, and delight in imagining themselves in new situations or experiences. The ability to stick to a main idea or see relationships and trends develops gradually during these years. (Check out the conversation of the fifth-graders in the next chapter as typical for this age group. You will note, while topics and ideas wander freely in and out, many ideas reflect considerable depth of thought.) These children, moving toward the brink of adult reasoning, are very much in need of adult models to show them what it is all about. And they are such fun to talk with! They should probably start with Level One, the easier questions, but may soon move on to more complex problems. Lovers of "law and order," they will relish being in charge of the discussion now and then.

AGES ELEVEN (OR TEN, OR TWELVE, OR THIRTEEN, OR SIXTEEN . . .) AND UP: In this age period, when individual timetables of maturation vary dramatically, young adolescents begin to refine their ideas about the world, to experiment with ethical thinking, and to gain new perspectives. They are particularly concerned about issues related to their own developing sense of identity, such as, "Why are some people cruel to others?" or "What would you do if you had to survive alone in the wilderness?" As they practice their newly objective attitudes—not only about ideas but about themselves and their parents—they may ask irritating questions and appear feisty and critical, experimenting with a new veneer of sophistication. No one denies they can be difficult, but what thoughts they have! This stage of pulling away from you—and your ideas—is essential for the growth of their own intellectual power. Grit your teeth and try to keep them involved; the rules for listening in the next chapter are particularly important for dealing successfully with teens. Level Two and Level Three questions can elicit fascinating discussions; the key is to convince them that you, too, are searching for answers and that you value their ideas. You might also let them know you appreciate the examples they set for younger brothers or sisters and give them frequent turns as discussion moderator. Everyone likes to feel important!

ADULTHOOD: Only recently have the "experts" acknowledged that people continue to change and mature cognitively even into or beyond their twenties. The final stage of intellectual maturity, now termed "problem-finding," takes place when we stop answering other people's questions and start generating our own. When you begin developing original open-ended questions, you are practicing—and modeling—this skill.

MODELING MATURE REASONING

Although we cannot expect children to think as adults do, we can certainly show them how! In the long run, the thinking patterns we demonstrate for children may be our most profound legacy, since their adult level of reasoning will be drawn in great part from these examples. Children who lack thoughtful models often develop problems when schoolwork begins to incorporate broad concepts and complex relationships such as "cause and effect" (If this happens . . . then what?). They also have difficulty figuring out how to approach new questions. One veteran fifth-grade social studies teacher recently told me, "I can sure tell the kids whose folks have talked with them about ideas—they have a whole different way of approaching the topics we study. So many of the others get upset if I don't tell them the answer right away because they don't know how to think about the idea themselves."

The questions in this book have been designed to help you provide these models. Most can accommodate both concrete and abstract interpretations, so even the youngest members of the family will soak up valuable skills as they tune in and participate. Your job is to help the conversation along, not only by contributing your own ideas but also by listening effectively to those of everyone else. Of course, in order to listen to children, we must first get them to talk. That's what the next chapter is all about.

─────── S I X ───────

DOES EAR WAX MAKE US HUMAN? CONVERSATIONAL TACTICS

' 'B ut my child doesn't want to talk!''
As most of us have discovered, children don't get into interesting conversations just because we want (or tell) them to! Even though the "Playful Ponderings" in Part Three are intrinsically appealing and stimulating, adults must still set up a constructive climate for conversation. Here are some principles and a sampling of useful phrases to keep in mind (these phrases and others are recapped for easy reference in "Talk Tactics" on pages 64–66):

1. *Give children air space* in which to express themselves. Remind yourself to hear the kids' ideas before voicing your own.

2. When a child (like anyone else) is talking, *give him or her your undivided attention.*

3. Make a real effort to *listen to the child's logic,* keeping in mind that it springs from a more concrete perspective

than yours. A *non sequitur* to you may be perfectly logical from the child's point of view.

4. *Ask questions* to clarify thinking, but be sure to use a *friendly tone of voice*, e.g.:

- "That's interesting; tell me more."

- "Why do you say that?"

- "Can you tell me a little more about . . . ?"

- "I don't quite understand what you mean . . ."

5. *Restate* what you think was said to clarify or expand, e.g.:

- "Are you saying . . . ?"

- "It sounds as if you're thinking [feeling] . . ."

- "If I understand you correctly, you're suggesting . . ."

- "You think . . . ?"

6. *Never, under any circumstances, ridicule or poke fun at a "childish" remark.* Even labeling comments "cute" is really no compliment to a child who is thinking as deeply as possible for his or her level of development. If you are truly listening,

you may discover some profound ideas hiding under the childish phrasing.

7. *Accept remarks even if you don't agree.*[1] While it is certainly reasonable to offer other points of view, we must be very gentle when dealing with children, who tend to feel their opinions are not as worthwhile as those of adults. Nonjudgmental acknowledgment keeps the pipeline of ideas open.

- "You make an interesting point . . ."

- "That's an idea I never heard before . . ."

- "You thought hard about that one . . ."

- "Here's another thought . . ."

8. After accepting an idea, it is all right to *challenge thinking* by demonstrating its logical extension—but do it tactfully and without sarcasm. Here is a brief excerpt from the conversation of a parent who was trying to extend his son Paul's thinking without criticizing his ideas:

The question under discussion was "When you eat an apple, is it alive?"

---

1. *These suggestions are made to open up the "conversation game" for the purposes of this book. I do not mean to imply that parents should never express disagreement with their children about real-life issues.*

Paul: Yes.

Dad: How do you know?

Paul: Well, it's juicy.

Dad: So, you're saying that being juicy makes something alive? What about a cherry pie? It's certainly juicy—is it alive? (clarifying thinking)

Paul: (giggling) No. Well . . . I don't think it's dead, anyway.

Dad: Well, I wonder how we know that something is alive. Maybe we should start with the apple on the tree. I think that's probably alive. Do you agree? (modeling another approach)

The trick here is to avoid putting yourself in an adversarial position; bear in mind that neither of you knows the answer.

9. *Don't put words in the child's mouth.* Stick to paraphrasing what he or she has said or to stating your own ideas, presented as such. (The one exception to this rule may occur in the case of a child who has difficulty with language expression, to be discussed shortly.)

10. If children get too far off the track, you may want to bring them back by *tactfully redirecting the conversation.*

- "That's really interesting. Let's go back to . . ."

- "Maybe we should talk about Mark's idea next time. I am still concerned about . . ."

All these techniques are effective, but they take a degree of practice. Don't be discouraged if your children's thinking does not immediately surge forth; time and patience are subtle lock pickers that will eventually release your children's ideas for you to appreciate.

DOES EAR WAX MAKE US HUMAN?

Here are three partial transcripts of discussions led by adults experienced in eliciting ideas from children. Note how these adult discussion guides subtly sum up, extend, and redirect the conversation, while still giving the youngsters relatively free rein in putting forth their ideas.

GRADE TWO:

Adult: Are you ready? Here's our question for today. What's a hero? How do you know someone is a hero?

Danny: Batman, Superman.

Bianca: It's someone who tries to like help someone.

Petey: I don't know any heroes . . .

Adult: Are you sure? Could your dad be a hero?

Chris: My dad is!

Petey: No, all he does is work. He's not a hero.

Adult: Bianca said a hero is someone who tries to help someone. Do you know anyone like that?

Bianca: Miss B.! (their teacher)

Adult: So is Miss B. a hero?

Chorus: No!— She's a *teacher*!

Adult: You mean you can't be a teacher and a hero at the same time?

Janey: Yes . . . Well, maybe . . . But she never has time to be a hero.

Ernie: Heroes try to save people. You have to save someone's life.

Chris: But there's this person on 911, he saves people's lives, but that's his job.

Adult: Chris raises a good question. If it's your job or you get paid for saving someone's life, are you still a hero? What about policemen and firemen?

GRADE FIVE:

Now let's look at a group of *fifth-graders* grappling with one of philosophy's oldest questions: What makes us human?

Adult: Imagine there's a robot standing in the middle of this room. What would we have to do to it, or add to it, so that we could call it human.

Christie: It would need skin and it wouldn't have to go around with batteries.

Sue: It would have to walk normally and talk normally.

Adult: So you're saying it would have to look like a human being? Then if you put a computer in there that would make it look and act like a human being, we could call it human?

Mike: If it needs to be programmed to do things, it can't be human.

Eric: You'd have to make it have—you know—a heart, blood, liver, brain, bones, hair . . .

Adult: Oh, so are there some special parts . . .

Danielle: (so excited she interrupts) But it still—it still didn't come from a human mommy!

Adult: You mean it wasn't born? Does that have something to do with it?

Trina: But I saw a thing about Robotos—they can like make a baby robot . . .

Mark: Wait . . . but it would have to do just like humans: go to the bathroom, have ear wax, nose hairs . . .

Sue: If it was made of metal or plastic, it would *not* be human.

Adult: But let's say a human got injured—maybe they had a bad heart or a bad liver, and the doctors put in a plastic substitute. Does that mean the person would no longer be human? At what point does he become a robot?

Mark: A human's a human; a robot's a robot!

Adult: But how can we tell the difference? Doctors can put in all sorts of bionic parts—where's the dividing line?

Renee: In the real bottom of his heart, he's not a robot.

58

Eric: And even if you made a robot look, you know, like a human, he wouldn't be.

Adult: Why not?

Eric: Because it isn't real.

Adult: What would make it more real?

Danielle: Well, the robot would have to have feelings. But maybe it would be like trying to change a Jewish person into a Christian.

Adult: Are you saying that the robot might not want to change into a human?

Eric: I think you should make a robot that can mate with a human.

Chorus: Oh, yuck . . .

Eric: Then you'd have a "hubot!"

(Laughter)

Adult: Maybe you'd have a "roman"—maybe the ancient "Romans" we were reading about were really half robots!

GRADE SEVEN:

Adult: Let's pretend you're walking out of your bedroom in the morning and you shut the door. Is your bed still there?

Tom: Of course, it is!

Adult: How do you know? Philosophers for years have

debated whether something exists if no one can see it, touch it, hear it, or sense it in any other way.

Charmayne: Oh, I get it. Maybe it isn't there. If you opened the door to look, then it would like be there again—but we can't tell . . .

Darlene: This is a spooky question!

Adult: Sam, you look like you have something to say . . .

Sam: Well, I think the bed's still there, but it's sort of like suspended matter—it's someplace between—between a real bed and an invisible bed, somewhere in between.

Elise: But my cat and dog sit on my bed when I'm gone. What would they do, drop to the floor—or just float there?

Adult: But if your cat and dog could see and feel the bed, it would be sensed, so we'd have to agree that it was there. What if they weren't in the room, though?

Elise: I don't like this question—it's making my head hurt with thinking.

Adult: Maybe your brain is growing, and that's what you're feeling.

Charmayne: This reminds me of another question I heard once. If a tree falls in the forest and no one hears it, does it make a sound . . . ?

Charles: Well, sound is air vibrations, so they're there whether you hear it or not.

Charmayne: But if nobody hears it, like what vibrates?

Maybe vibrations don't vibrate if they don't hit anything . . .

So, there's our snippet of intellectual inquiry from the
younger set. Notice how the adults extended, clarified, and
brought up new ideas without taking over the discussion or
pushing for premature "answers." That—along with an interesting question—is the secret to getting kids to talk!

HOW TO HELP A CHILD WHO HAS TROUBLE
WITH LANGUAGE EXPRESSION

Some youngsters have great ideas but genuine difficulty lining
up words to express them. These youngsters can be helped
in several ways:

1. A child with an expressive language difficulty needs
more air space than anyone else. If necessary, fend off the
verbal tigers with a large (figurative) stick to ensure he or she
has all the time needed to organize ideas into sentences.

2. You will need to be an excellent listener and try to
divine what the child wants to say. This is your hardest job.

3. Model and help frame a sentence to express the idea.
You may need to, quite literally, put words in a child's mouth
to get the thought into manageable form.

4. Acknowledge and praise any grammatically reasonable
version of the idea, even if it seems immature in terms of the

child's real age. By all means, do not let anyone make fun of this child.

5. Many children also experience "word-finding" problems that make it difficult for them to think quickly of nouns and verbs (aging brains have this difficulty, too, as some of us are discovering!). Encourage them to take the time to think of a real word instead of a "filler" ("stuff," "you know," "the thingy," etc.). First-letter clues also help: "Does the word you're thinking of begin with a 'g'?"

During the fifth-grade discussion described previously, one boy sat fidgeting noticeably. Eventually he began to jump around and make semiguttural sounds. The adult recognized him, giving his classmates a clear message to be quiet.

"Evan, I can tell you've got an important idea in there. Give it a shot."

"Well, um, um, the robot . . . coming with . . . well, it hasn't got . . . the human comes . . . you know . . . brain!" shouted Evan.

"Slow down, Evan." (The guide has inferred what Evan is trying to say and will now attempt to help him frame a sentence.) "Are you saying, 'The human has something the robot doesn't? The human has a . . .' Go on, say it, Evan."

"Yeah, the human has a . . . a . . . a brain!"

"And the robot doesn't?"

"Yeah. And the robot doesn't! Not real, really, yeah!"

"That's an important thought, Evan. Does anyone want to say more about that?"

Physical restlessness or habits of misbehavior often mask the frustration experienced by a nonverbal thinker, and special help should be sought from reputable language therapists for these youngsters. We can also help at home and in the regular classroom if we are patient and firm in helping the child express thoughts.

For all children, wise coaches act as bridges between unformed ideas and mutual understanding. That's what this "conversation game" is all about.

TALK TACTICS
Helpful Phrases for Extending Conversations

Acknowledging

- "That's a new idea."

- "You really thought about that one."

- "I see."

- "Interesting."

- "Denise raises an interesting point . . ."

Restating

- "You're wondering if . . . ?"

- "You want to know . . . ?"

- "Does that mean . . . ?"

- "Are you saying . . . ?"

- "It sounds as if you're thinking [feeling] . . ."

- "If I understand you correctly, you're suggesting . . ."

- "You think . . . ?"

- "So you're disagreeing with . . . ?"

Clarifying

- "That's interesting; tell me more."

- "Why do you say that?"

- "Can you tell me a little more about . . . ?"

- "I don't quite understand what you mean . . ."

- "What are we really discussing here?"

- "That seems to relate to what Joe just said."

- "Let me understand better what you're saying . . ."

Disagreeing

- You make an interesting point; have you considered . . . ?"

- "That's an idea I never heard before . . ."

- "You thought hard about that one but is it possible that . . ."

- "Here's another thought . . . ?"

- "One problem I have when I think about this idea is . . ."

Challenging Thinking

- "I wonder how we know . . . ?"

- "If that is true, then is . . . also true?"

- "Can you give us some reasons for . . . ?"

Redirecting

- "How does that relate to what Jeanne just said?"

- "Maybe we should talk about that idea next time. I am still concerned about . . ."

- "Interesting idea. Let's go back to . . ."

- "Nice point, but we hadn't finished discussing . . ."

Expanding

- "I wonder what anyone else is thinking about this . . . ?"

Part Three

PLAYFUL
PONDERINGS

H O W T O P L A Y T H E
C O N V E R S A T I O N G A M E

*C*onversations sparked by the open-ended questions on
the following pages have some practical advantages:

- They don't cost anything.

- They don't require any fancy equipment (other than
  your brains, of course).

- They are completely portable.

- They don't need to take a lot of time.

FINDING THE TIME

After a little practice you will find that interesting ideas slide
readily into nooks and crannies of even the most peripatetic
lives. I have had some of my most intriguing conversations
with children in less than twenty minutes and in some very
peculiar places. With some topics, of course, you may be
inspired to continue longer or take up the idea at another
time, but quality here is definitely more important than

quantity! Here are some golden, but often overlooked opportunities:

- carpools
- en route to and waiting for doctor's and dentist's appointments
- dining at McDonald's
- mealtimes at home
- family or school trips and outings
- classroom "downtime"; between activities or even as a period scheduled for "thinking skills"

GETTING STARTED

In order to use this book most effectively, you may want to present questions as a "conversation game." Your job includes setting the stage, mastering and explaining the ground rules, and helping participants practice positive habits so that everyone has fun. Here's how to do it:

STEP ONE: SET THE STAGE It is sad, but true, that many of us have such dreadful conversational patterns with our children that we need to unlearn old habits and establish new ones. Please, do not become discouraged if sparkling dialogue does not immediately spring up around your dinner table! New patterns take time to develop, but presenting them in a game format makes change more palatable. Most of the suggestions below are common-sense ones that need little elaboration.

Guidelines:

1. *Make it clear to your children that talking with them is* a priority *for you.* Their positive participation will hinge directly on your attitudes and expectations. One father got a regular substitute for one of his biweekly tennis games so he could dine—and talk—with his kids. Not surprisingly, they bought into the plan with enthusiasm.

2. *Set aside time when no interruptions will be permitted.* Each family has its own method of approaching this challenge. Solutions depend somewhat on the previous level of organization of family time together. A busy mom who always wrings the maximum out of every minute decided to schedule "time for conversation" on her Filofax, conferring instant status on this activity in her children's eyes. Some parents prefer to fit discussion times into a regular routine, such as a normally scheduled mealtime or lull in weekend activities. Whatever your group's style, I suggest you start by setting aside a *fifteen- to thirty-minute block of time once a week* (if everyone wants more, great, but don't force it). With older children,

it is important to consult with them so this activity will not conflict with any major obligations. Absolutely no telephone conversations, television, or other nonlife-threatening interruptions should be permitted—and this includes adults as well as children. ("I'm sorry, Paul, we're in the midst of a family conversation. May I ask Mark to call you back in thirty minutes?") If the children balk despite your best efforts to enlist their cooperation, go ahead and assert your parental prerogatives. They will probably come around if they find the topics interesting and realize they won't be put on the spot. Try letting one of them choose the question to be discussed.

3. *Mealtimes lend themselves well to relaxed conversation, but weekday breakfast time is not an ideal time to promote thinking skills.* Several families I know have found that scheduling one specific dinnertime per week purely for this activity is the best way to start. (Some also make this meal a bit more formal than usual, with candles on the table, menu especially planned and/or prepared by the children, etc.) One concerned set of parents told me, however, that the only time they were all at home together was at breakfast. Understandably, they were finding it difficult to engage anyone's attention; recalling the early morning scenes in our household, I could easily understand their predicament. They finally settled on a leisurely Sunday brunch conversation time.

4. *Let your children know from the outset that you are eager to hear*

their ideas—and mean it! ("I've just gotten this book that has some very intriguing [interesting, weird] questions in it. I'd really be interested in hearing what everyone has to say about some of these ideas!") A parent's (or teacher's) genuine interest in what a child or teenager has to say is a seductive commodity for any youngster. *Warning:* If your children have learned to expect far more lecturing than listening from the adults in their lives, it may take several positive experiences to rebuild their confidence!

5. *Keep it* fun *and leave them wanting more.* Playing with ideas—including serious ones—can be a pleasant, even lighthearted adventure. If you try to turn these conversations into lesson time, your children will soon decide they want nothing to do with them—or with you! Do not prolong your discussions if everyone is fidgeting and rolling their eyes with boredom. Your main objective is to keep the dialogue sufficiently interesting and lively to inspire repeat events. If ten minutes exhausts one topic, drop it. You will doubtless find, as I have, that consistent practice with these techniques gradually increases both the quantity and quality of the dialogue. In fact, you may be amazed how little time it takes before you notice new depths in your children's reasoning.

STEP TWO: EXPLAIN THE GROUND RULES This step and the following one are the most critical aspects of the whole adventure. Try hard to structure the situation so each participant feels (1) safe to express ideas and (2) obliged to listen to others. If these habits have not been previously established, be firm in insisting everyone turn over a new leaf. This practice in good conversational habits alone will be well worth all your effort!

Ground Rules:

1. *Everyone's ideas are equally worthwhile.* Make it clear at the outset that these questions have *no right answers.* Point out that you are no more of an expert than anyone else.

2. *Suspend judgment: nothing is "right" or "wrong."* These words should be off-limits. I recommend you also avoid such phrases as, "Good idea!" if you can (it's harder than you might think) because it implies a judgment, i.e., other ideas might be not as good or just plain bad. The list of "Talk Tactics" in the previous chapter offers nonjudgmental alternatives.

3. *One person will act as facilitator or conversation guide.* You should assume this role at first, but children can eventually be encouraged to guide the discussion. The job of the facilitator is simply to keep things moving, not to dictate.

4. *No one is allowed to make fun of or put down anyone else or his or her ideas. Period!* If you explain this rule assertively and immediately squelch any such behavior if it occurs, most children will respect the underlying principle. After all, it

means they are safe from embarrassment, too. Adults, of course, will realize this rule goes double for them.

5. *No interrupting, when someone else is talking.* If one person is clearly monopolizing the floor, the facilitator should tactfully suggest that he or she summarize the point.

6. Everyone should *give the speaker their attention,* and try to listen and understand what is being said. The facilitator may periodically *ask someone to summarize or rephrase what another person said* before stating a new thought. This ploy encourages better listening habits as well as the ability to synthesize ideas; try to make it an increasingly important part of your group's process.

Warning: Many children—and adults—in today's inattentive world will have difficulty with the above request. If so, ask the first person to restate the point and try again. If person number two still cannot rephrase it, drop the issue or let someone else try. Simply calling attention to the importance of listening in specific ways will tend to improve habits over time. Of course, it would be ridiculous to ask a seven-year-old or a child who has trouble with verbal expression to summarize a complex point made by an older person. Follow your common sense. Remember, above all, we want this to be *fun!*

7. *If people disagree, they must do so politely,* with words (no poking or kicking under the table).

Edward deBono, one of the gurus in "thinking skills"

research, stresses the difference between the *adversary position* in conversation (I'm right, you're wrong, and I'll now prove it to you) and what he calls *"joint exploration" of ideas*. Most of us have been well-indoctrinated in the former, but it is this latter quality we seek to cultivate. Set up a nonjudgmental atmosphere and watch ideas emerge, grow, branch, and flourish.

POSITIVE	NO-NO'S
"That's an interesting point, but . . ."	"That's a dumb idea!"
I understand what you're saying, but . . ."	"You're wrong."
"What makes you say that?"	"How could you ever think that?"
"I'm not sure I understand . . ."	"No one could believe such a thing."

8. *Avoid external authorities during discussion.* If you are tempted immediately to reach for a dictionary or encyclopedia, resist the impulse. The purpose is to expand thinking by considering new ideas before recapitulating old ones. Of course, if children's curiosity is sufficiently stimulated so that later on they start digging into reference books, no one is going to complain!

STEP THREE: THROW THE CONVERSATIONAL BALL—AND HELP IT ROLL After the ground rules have been clearly set forth, the facilitator selects a question and reads it. It is best to start with Level One unless you are dealing exclusively with teenagers and adults who might enjoy Level Two questions. A good entrée into most children's imaginations is: "If you had only one wish . . ." Another easy starter is "If you could spend one day as an animal . . ." Middle-school children respond well to "If you had a time machine and could go forward or backward . . ." (See the next section for specific wording.) Pick one that you think will interest your group. Use the hints that accompany the questions if you need them. Let the ideas run as long as you wish; if they diverge somewhat from the main topic, steer it gently back, but don't worry as long as the discussion is lively and interesting. Again, *the purpose is not to answer the question, but to stimulate thinking.* Your ideas, of course, are important too. One trick is to phrase them as questions, e.g., "*I wonder* if having all my wishes come true might get confusing . . . ?" rather than, "*I think* having all my wishes come true would . . ."

STEP FOUR: ENFORCE THE GROUND RULES AND DEAL WITH PROBLEMS Creativity in expression does not imply anarchy. Adults must insist that positive habits are demonstrated and followed. Most children will cooperate, given a minimum of firm guidance; occasionally, however, problems surface that have much deeper roots and should be dealt with directly.

1. *The uncooperative one.* If a child consistently misbehaves or purposely "bugs" others to get attention, sit down with him or her privately and discuss the situation rather than trying to discipline in front of everyone else. Try to elicit some reasons for the misbehavior, using the listening skills already discussed. Make a clear and affectionate statement to the effect that you really want this youngster to be a constructive part of the group. You may need to suggest a brief "time-out" period: the child leaves the room until he or she feels able to return and participate constructively. Permanently excluding a troublesome family member only exacerbates the problem. If you're absolutely stymied, seek some outside help. Do not let this situation continue unattended, however, as such negative habits tend to get worse the longer they go on.

2. *The clam.* In any group, and usually in any family, there is at least one shy child who prefers observing to participating. Such youngsters may have an expressive language problem that needs attention. On the other hand, they may have excellent language skills but simply choose not to use them. They may have been intimidated by being "put down" in previous conversations, or they may just have "observers'" temperaments. Since this temperamental style, sometimes

termed "slow to warm up," has been noted even in infants, it may be difficult to change. If a child is able to express ideas clearly but elects to remain on the sidelines of a conversation, I would suggest you not press the issue. I personally believe that children should not be forced to participate if they clearly prefer roles as listeners. Occasionally try asking for a comment ("Susie, I know you always have some interesting ideas; do you want to say anything?" or "Michael, we'd love to hear from you . . ."), but if the decision is "No," let it rest. If Susie or Michael makes a move to speak, however, be sure the airways are cleared and immediate positive recognition is given for this effort to participate.

3. *Cain and Abel.* Most brothers and sisters have latent and overt antagonism for each other coursing through their tender little veins—and it sometimes gushes forth at the most awkward moments! Households placing great stress on competition tend to exacerbate this problem. Emphasizing and maintaining the noncompetitive aspects of this format will help pave the way toward more peaceable habits. If you give these ground rules a firm and extended trial, however, and two or more children are so overtly hostile toward each other that they are ruining it for everyone, you might as well admit you have a bigger problem and seek some help. Books (see Bibliography for examples) are now available with positive guidelines for dealing with sibling rivalry, and/or you might decide to seek some professional counseling before you have to lock them (or yourself?) into separate cages.

4. *The wiggly ones.* Some children (and some adults) have genuine difficulty sitting still for twenty minutes. If you have a wiggly type, allow the child to get up and move about as long as he stays in the room and tries not to disrupt the conversation. Some lenience in this regard is important because many young children need to move their bodies in order to express their ideas, a normal function of a developing nervous system. If a child is so rapt in expressing a thought that she twines herself around a chair as though it were a set of monkey bars, I am inclined to overlook the gymnastics and go for the ideas. Again, adult judgment will make the final call in each situation.

STEP FIVE: USE PROVEN CONVERSATIONAL GAMBITS TO KEEP THE TOPIC ALIVE A number of techniques now taught in communications courses are useful at home and in the classroom. Here's a sampling:

1. If the question seems unclear, reword it. There is nothing sacrosanct about the way these particular questions are phrased; their purpose is to elicit discussion, not quibble over semantics.

2. Try brainstorming if your group has difficulty coming up with ideas. Many people are already familiar with the rules, which are explained in the box on p. 83.

3. Give participants time and space to express themselves. Keep older children from overriding the thoughts of younger

ones. Your firm attitude of mutual respect will be an important guide.

4. Suspend excessive analysis of ideas. Logic and analysis are valuable skills, but they may narrow thinking if they come too soon in these conversations. Your purpose is to elicit and guide, rather than dissect ideas.

5. If children's responses seem illogical to your adult mind, listen carefully and try to understand what the child is really saying.

6. Remember these steps to keep the discussion moving:

- listen (eye contact and body posture convey your interest)

- acknowledge (e.g., "Yes, that is an interesting suggestion . . .")

- rephrase (e.g., "If I understood you, you said . . .")

7. Encourage the thinking process instead of praising children's remarks (this is difficult!). Rather than saying, "What a great idea!" you might try to comment on the child's effort instead.

- "You really thought hard about that one."

- "I like the way you thought that idea through."

- "You really listened well to what Mary said."

- "Thanks for listening so carefully to my idea."

STEP SIX: FOLLOW UP 1. Read a book out loud and encourage discussion of the ideas. (Jim Trelease's *New Read-Aloud Handbook* is a good guidebook.) With many questions I have included titles of "Read-Alouds": books whose themes are at least tangentially related. They won't provide answers, but they will help elaborate the ideas and extend the conversation. Now is also the time to seek out dictionaries, encyclopedias, and other reference books, if curiosity has been piqued by the discussion.

2. Children and adults alike will benefit from an opportunity to reflect on the issues raised. Brains need "downtime" to assimilate learning and firm up new ways of thinking. My personal hope is that these "playful ponderings" will reveal some enticing new mental vistas for each of you. They may even make the habit of creative inquiry so enjoyable as to open up new ways of approaching whatever questions life presents.

And Now for the Fun! . . .

HOW TO "BRAINSTORM"

Guidelines:

• Explain that you are trying to get as many ideas as possible out on the table in a short amount of time.

• Present the question or problem and invite participants to contribute ideas. Reassure them that no one will judge or comment on their suggestions, so they may give their imaginations free rein.

• Anyone can offer an idea, no matter how strange or off-base.

• No explanations, questions, or judgments allowed. These steps should be saved for later.

Procedures:

• Let ideas flow as rapidly as possible; you will find they tend to "feed" off each other and become more interesting as you go along.

• After the outpouring has diminished, or at the end of a given time period, end the brainstorming session. Go back and pick up on suggestions the group finds interesting.

• Now is the time for questions ("What did you mean by . . ."), explanations, and comments.

~~~~~~~ E I G H T ~~~~~~~

MIND-OPENERS,
MIND-STRETCHERS,
AND MIND-BOGGLERS

LEVEL ONE

Mind-Openers

These questions are appropriate for primary-aged children (through Grade Three) and as "starters" for older ones of any age. They concern concrete objects and experiences to which the child can personally relate. Tugging on the imagination, they encourage the use of visual imagery (making "mind pictures") and thinking about familiar things—or themselves—in unfamiliar settings. Interacting with adults and older children on Level One questions gradually pulls young ones toward more abstract forms of reasoning.

"Read-Alouds," when included, will help provide concrete examples. I have tried to recommend books that are interesting and age-appropriate for each level, but because children vary so dramatically in their interests and understanding (e.g., some seven-year-olds are captivated by books that are beyond the reach of some ten-year-olds) adult judgment is advised. Your librarian can be a helpful resource, and there is nothing wrong with "sampling" several books to find one your family really enjoys, whatever its "age level."

Follow-up questions and hints are also included, with some questions to help you get started. After a little practice, you'll undoubtedly start developing your own.

If you had only one wish—and you couldn't ask for any more wishes, what would you wish?

HINT: After everyone has had a chance to think and express a wish, try probing gently about the implications of what they have wished. For example:

"*I'd wish to win the lottery.*"

Question: "What would you do with all that money? Do you think it would make you happy?"

"*I'd wish to be magic.*"

Question: "What does it mean to be "magic"? What would you be able to do that you can't do now? What might happen at school—at home, etc.?"

FOLLOW-UP QUESTION: *What do you think your life would be like if you could have all the wishes you ever wanted?*

READ-ALOUD

Brittain, Bill. WISH GIVER.

Catling, Patrick Skene. THE CHOCOLATE TOUCH.

Eager, Edward. HALF MAGIC.

Hutchins, Hazel J. THE THREE AND MANY WISHES OF JASON REED.

Selden, George. GENIE OF SUTTON PLACE.

Steig, William. SYLVESTER AND THE MAGIC PEBBLE.

Zemach, Margot (from the GRIMM BROTHERS). THE FISHERMAN AND HIS WIFE.

Pretend you have a magic pair of wings in your closet that will take you anywhere you want to go. Where would you like to fly?

FOLLOW-UP QUESTIONS: *What would you take with you? What might you do when you got there?*

READ-ALOUD
Hughes, Shirley. UP AND UP.
Ryder, Joanne. NIGHT FLIGHT.

If you could spend one day as an animal, which one would you choose to be? Tell about what you think your day might be like.

HINT: Young children may need a little prompting or some examples from older folks to help them envision life from an animal's perspective.

READ-ALOUD

There are hundreds of children's books about animals. These four are among many good ones for reading aloud.

Kipling, Rudyard. JUST SO STORIES and THE JUNGLE BOOK.

Lewis, J. Patrick. A HIPPOPOTAMUSN'T. (verse)

Parker, Arthur. SKUNNY WUNDY: SENECA INDIAN TALES.

Would you like to have the power to become invisible whenever you wanted to? When might you choose to become invisible? What do you think would happen?

T_{ry} *to imagine what your life would be like if you were the size of a mouse.*

HINT: By attempting to put themselves into another's point of view, children develop important reasoning skills. They may need help from adults or older children in "seeing" the world from a different perspective. Actually getting down on the floor and looking up is one way to develop a new point of view!

FOLLOW-UP QUESTIONS: *What things could you do that you can't do now? What things couldn't you do?*

READ-ALOUD

Banks, Lynn Reid. THE INDIAN IN THE CUPBOARD.

Cleary, Beverly. THE MOUSE AND THE MOTORCYCLE.

Lionni, Leo. FREDERICK.

Norton, Mary. THE BORROWERS.

Peterson, John. THE LITTLES.

Pratchett, Terry. TRUCKERS and DIGGERS.

White, E. B. STUART LITTLE.

Imagine the most special birthday party you can.

FOLLOW-UP QUESTION: *Now think about how you might have a very special birthday party without spending any money.*

READ-ALOUD

Bunting, Eve. THE WEDNESDAY SURPRISE.

Willard, Nancy. THE HIGH RISE GLORIOUS SKITTLE SKAT RORIOUS SKY PIE ANGEL FOOD CAKE.

How do you know you're angry?

HINT: Since all children (as well as the rest of us) have angry feelings at times, it is often constructive to acknowledge and discuss them. You might also want to share ideas about what you do when you do get angry.

FOLLOW-UP QUESTIONS: *What makes you angry? Why? What if no one in the world ever got angry? (A more abstract question: harder for young children to grapple with.)*

READ-ALOUD
Simon, Norma. I WAS SO MAD!
Zolotow, Charlotte. THE HATING BOOK.

What is the scariest thing that ever happened to you? What made it so scary?

FOLLOW-UP QUESTION: *What do you do when you're scared?*

READ-ALOUD

Berkey, Barry and Velma. ROBBERS, BONES, AND MEAN DOGS.

Dagliesh, Alice. THE BEARS ON HEMLOCK MOUNTAIN.

Martin, Bill. THE GHOST-EYED TREE.

Prelutsky, Jack. NIGHTMARES: POEMS TO TROUBLE YOUR SLEEP.

Schwartz, Alvin. IN A DARK, DARK ROOM AND OTHER SCARY STORIES.

————. SCARY STORIES TO TELL IN THE DARK. (may be too scary for some younger ones)

What is an adventure?

FOLLOW-UP QUESTIONS: *Why is an adventure different from other experiences? What is your most recent adventure?*

READ-ALOUD

There are, of course, hundreds of good adventure books for reading aloud. Here is a sampling:

Baum, L. Frank. THE WONDERFUL WIZARD OF OZ.

Browne, Anthony. GORILLA.

Bunting, Eve. HOW MANY DAYS TO AMERICA?

Collodi, Carlo. THE ADVENTURES OF PINOCCHIO.

Gannett, Ruth. MY FATHER'S DRAGON.

Holling, Holling C. PADDLE-TO-THE-SEA. (an oldie; may be hard to find)

Schertle, Alice. IN MY TREEHOUSE.

Willard, Nancy. SAILING TO CYTHERA AND OTHER ANATOLE STORIES.

What is the most delicious thing you can imagine?

HINT: Using words in varied contexts helps children expand important reasoning skills. Many children with language problems have difficulty with this sort of question, so tread easily if they do not immediately pick up on the idea. Your examples will be very important in showing them how.

FOLLOW-UP QUESTIONS: *What might be delicious other than food? Can you think of*
   a delicious feeling
   a delicious experience
   a delicious place

READ-ALOUD
Babbit, Natalie. THE SEARCH FOR DELICIOUS.
Barrett, Judi. CLOUDY WITH A CHANCE OF MEATBALLS.

How *ow many things can you think of that are*

strong
soft
light
free

HINT: Here's another question to build understanding of abstract word meanings. You might make a game of thinking of other words that fall into this category.

How can you tell that someone is your friend? What do you need to do to be a friend?

HINT: See if you can get beyond the usual "Being nice" response to some more specific qualities: e.g., "What does 'nice' mean? What do people do that shows they are 'nice.' " "If people are nice, does that mean they are automatically your friends?"

FOLLOW-UP QUESTION: *What is the most important thing about being a friend?*

READ-ALOUD

Clifton, Lucille. MY FRIEND JACOB.

Morey, Walt. GENTLE BEN.

Sleishman, Sid. THE WHIPPING BOY.

Steig, William. AMOS AND BORIS.

White, E. B. CHARLOTTE'S WEB.

If you had the choice, where would you prefer to live: the city, the suburbs, a small town, or the country?

HINT: Many elementary students do not have a clear idea of these differences, nor of the terms "urban," "suburban," and "rural." When you talk about them, you will be building vocabulary and categorization skills as well as broadening outlooks. You might approach this question by brainstorming the advantages and disadvantages of each type of environment.

READ-ALOUD

Burton, Virginia. THE LITTLE HOUSE.

Hopkins, Lee Bennett. THIS STREET'S FOR ME.

Isadoro, Rachel. BEN'S TRUMPET.

Levoy, Myron. THE WITCH OF FOURTH STREET.

Selden, George. THE CRICKET IN TIMES SQUARE.

I*f you could invent a magic potion that would change any person you know in any way you wanted to, who would you use it on first? Why? If you could take it yourself, would you?*

READ-ALOUD

Coville, Bruce. THE MONSTER'S RING.

Mayer, Marianna. SORCERER'S APPRENTICE.

What if you found a secret passage in your house or apartment?

FOLLOW-UP QUESTIONS: *Where might it go? What if it were a magical passage—what kinds of adventures would you like to have?*

READ-ALOUD

Lewis, C. S. THE LION, THE WITCH, AND THE WARDROBE.

If you could talk to animals, what would you try to find out?

FOLLOW-UP QUESTIONS: *What animal would you most like to talk to? Do you think animals can talk to each other? How?*

READ-ALOUD

Davis, Deborah. SECRET OF THE SEAL.

Lawson, Robert. RABBIT HILL.

Lofting, Hugh. THE STORY OF DR. DOLITTLE. (new edition)

If you could put all the boring things in the world into a box and close it up tight, do you think you would ever open it up again?

HINT: Try listing all the boring things everyone can think of. Your discussion may reveal that not everyone agrees what constitutes "boring." This exploration of others' attitudes is a good mind-stretcher. The question is reminiscent of the myth of "Pandora's Box," which can be found in *D'Aulaires' Book of Greek Myths*, the *Macmillan Book of Greek Gods and Heroes* by Arvis Stewart, or other good mythology sources.

If you were Grand Ruler of All Schools, how would you change yours?

HINT: This question offers a golden opportunity for adults (including grandparents) and children to exchange information about a very important part of their lives, as it provides a springboard for recounting memories, funny anecdotes, and even embarrassing experiences from everyone's school days. You might like to try a little "compare and contrast" by finding similarities and differences between schools nowadays and those in previous times. Your children will be delighted!

READ-ALOUD

Brink, Carol. CADDIE WOODLAWN.

DeJong, Meindert. WHEEL ON THE SCHOOL.

Hausherr, Rosmarie. ONE-ROOM SCHOOL AT SQUABBLE HOLLOW.

Stevenson, James. THAT DREADFUL DAY.

Wilder, Laura Ingalls. LITTLE HOUSE series.

How many things can you think of to do with a balloon?

HINT: This type of question is used in courses on "creativity" to encourage fluidity and flexibility of thinking. To get started, you might speculate about balloons of different sizes, materials, etc. Brainstorming is a particularly good technique for questions of this type. Then try imagining types of balloons you've never seen—or that have not yet been invented.

READ-ALOUD

Coxe, Molly. LOUELLA AND THE YELLOW BALLOON.

Levoy, Myron. THE MAGIC HAT OF MORTIMER WINTERGREEN.

P;agene duBois, William. THE TWENTY-ONE BALLOONS.

Scarry, Huck. BALLOON TRIP.

Zubrowski, Bernie. BALLOONS: BUILDING AND EXPERIMENTING WITH INFLATABLE TOYS.

What would you do if you walked into your kitchen tomorrow morning and found a real, live unicorn standing there?

FOLLOW-UP QUESTION: *What other unusual things can you think of that might cause a stir if they turned up in your kitchen?*

READ-ALOUD

Edwards, Patricia Kier. CHESTER AND UNCLE WILLOUGHBY.

Lindbergh, Reeve. THE DAY THE GOOSE GOT LOOSE.

Waber, Bernard. THE HOUSE ON EAST EIGHTY-EIGHTH STREET

What *if you had a magic paintbrush that would make whatever you painted come alive. What would you paint?*

HINT: This question was purposely left open-ended in terms of what could get painted. Different children envision this question in different ways, so let them express whatever ideas they have without imposing too many of your own. After some discussion, which will probably suggest some problems that could occur, you might ask, "Now that we've thought about this, let me ask—should you keep this paintbrush or bury it forever in a dark cavern?"

READ-ALOUD

Agee, Jon. THE INCREDIBLE PAINTING OF FELIX CLOUSSEAU.

Tresselt, Alvin. MA LIEN AND THE MAGIC BRUSH.

Zadrynska, Eva. THE GIRL WITH A WATERING CAN.

D_o *you think it would be a good idea if everyone had* *to wear a badge showing what kind of mood they were* *in?*

HINT: Children often say they would like to know what mood their teacher is in. You might ask, for example, "If Mr. X had on a bad-mood badge, what could you do to change it?"

FOLLOW-UP QUESTIONS: *What kind of badge might you have* *worn today? How might it have made your day different?*

H*ow do you remember different things? For example:*

a list of things to buy at the store
how to swim
how to find your way home
how to spell "vacation"
what the word "vacation" means
the place where you went on your last vacation

HINT: Research shows that children develop good memories partially as a result of being exposed to adults who talk about the importance of remembering things and show the children how they do it themselves. Simply calling attention to the many different types of memory, as these items do, is important for young children. Most will reply (and you may, too), "I just do!" Try to get beyond that into some specific strategies. You will find a lot of individual variation here—and remember, no one's way is the *right* way.

What makes someone a hero or heroine?

HINT: These questions may be too difficult for some seven-year-olds. It's up to you whether you want to get into the differences in common perceptions of the terms "hero" and "heroine."

FOLLOW-UP QUESTIONS: *Do you know anyone whom you consider a hero or heroine? Why?*

Have you ever done anything brave? Is it always good to be brave? Do you have to face danger to be a hero? Could someone be a hero and still run away from danger?

READ-ALOUD

Many classic children's books offer a good follow-up for this discussion. A few particularly good ones for fairly mature listeners:

Alexander, Lloyd. THE BOOK OF THREE and others in the Prydain Chronicles series.

Burt, Olive. BLACK WOMEN OF VALOR.

Cleaver, Vera and Bill. WHERE THE LILIES BLOOM.

Flack, Marjorie. THE COUNTRY BUNNY AND THE LITTLE GOLD SHOES. (for younger ones, up to age 8)

Lewis, C. S. THE LION, THE WITCH, AND THE WARDROBE and others in the Narnia Chronicles series.

O'Dell, Scott. SING DOWN THE MOON.

Yolen, Jane. ACORN QUEST.

Why do things look smaller when they are far away?

FOLLOW-UP QUESTION: *Do people on airplanes shrink when they go 'way up in the air? How can you tell?*

READ-ALOUD
Thurber, James. MANY MOONS.

LEVEL TWO

Mind-Stretchers

This level is aimed at youngsters from approximately third grade through adolescence. Younger ones should first warm up with Level One. These questions, as well as the "Read-Alouds," are designed to accommodate wide variations in mental maturity, and younger children will profit from hearing the ideas of adults and teens as well as from exploring and expressing their own thoughts. They will have to "step outside" their personal perspective, imagine new scenarios, and connect seemingly unrelated ideas—mind-stretchers at any age!

(Note: You will find several different varieties of questions in this section because some youngsters who draw an absolute blank on some types of questions respond immediately to another sort. Thus I have tried to include a wide range to appeal to everyone's personal "style.")

Imagine that when you wake up tomorrow morning everything in the world is yellow.

FOLLOW-UP QUESTIONS: *How would your day be different? Can you foresee what problems this might cause in the world? Would any new laws be needed? New products?*

D*esign the perfect house pet. What would you name it?*

READ-ALOUD

Atwater, Richard and Florence. MR. POPPER'S PENGUINS.

Pinkwater, Daniel. THE HOBOKEN CHICKEN EMERGENCY.

What might happen if people suddenly developed the ability to breathe underwater as well as to breathe air?

FOLLOW-UP QUESTION: *How might this development change the world as we know it?*

READ-ALOUD

Andersen, Hans Christian. THE LITTLE MERMAID.

If a TV reporter were standing outside our window looking in right now, what kind of a story might she come up with as she watches us having this discussion?

One father answered this question without hesitation. "Children Talk with Parents—that's news!" he exclaimed. Perhaps you can take it a little farther . . .

Imagine a world in which everyone looked alike.

HINT: Assume, although people all have the same physical appearance, that natural age differences will show: e.g., All newborns will look the same, all five-year-olds, all thirty-year-olds, etc. Maybe you can figure out a different way to envision this question.

FOLLOW-UP QUESTIONS: *Which of our familiar customs would have to be changed? What new products might we need to invent? What would schools have to do differently?*

Why is it important to keep a secret?

HINT: To add to this conversation, you may want to bring up a question that touches on a powerful ethical issue: What if a friend told you a secret, but you knew that if you kept the secret someone else would be hurt?

READ-ALOUD
Baur, Marian Dane. ON MY HONOR.
Fritz, Jean. BRADY.

H_{ow} *would the world be different if people were born with wheels instead of feet?*

HINT: If you need to, ask about possible differences in houses, cars, streets, clothing, etc.

READ-ALOUD
Silverstein, Shel. THE LIGHT IN THE ATTIC.

Why do you think people do mean things to other people?

READ-ALOUD

A few provocative books from among many possibilities.

Hooks, William. MEAN JAKE AND THE DEVILS.

Kherdian, David. THE ROAD FROM HOME.

Merrill, Jean. THE PUSHCART WAR.

Taylor, Mildred. ROLL OF THUNDER, HEAR MY CRY.

You have been assigned the project of coming up with a new design for houses for the twenty-first century. You may add, change, or eliminate rooms, change exterior structure, change building materials, or change anything else you choose.

HINT: Let your imaginations run wild; brainstorming is once more a good way to begin.

READ-ALOUD
Isaacson, Philip M. ROUND BUILDINGS, SQUARE BUILDINGS, AND BUILDINGS THAT WIGGLE LIKE A FISH.

If *you were boss of all television programs, what kind of programs would you show?*

HINT: You may well find yourself discussing some value-laden issues here: e.g., Would you allow violent programs—and where would you draw the line? What should preschoolers watch? What kind of news reporting is best? Would you use docudrama? Children have interesting and relevant opinions on these issues.

Can *you imagine what the location of your home will look like fifty years in the future? One hundred years? One thousand years'?*

HINT: On this follow-up question I broke my own rules; it is a convergent question—just in case you're starting to hunger for some "right answers." You can imagine the historical setting, or take a trip to the history book (a good one for middle grades and older is *The Landmark History of the American People* by Daniel J. Boorstin), but good historical novels about your section of the country may inspire more imagination. Check with your local librarian or consult one of the reference books for children's literature listed in the Bibliography. Remember that elementary-age children have a great deal of trouble envisioning historical time—either forward or backward. Creating a "time line" with dates and events depicted in chronological order helps everyone grasp these difficult concepts.

FOLLOW-UP QUESTION: *What do you think it looked like fifty, one hundred, or one thousand years in the past?*

S*hould schools give grades? Why or why not?*

FOLLOW-UP QUESTIONS: *What advantages do grades have? What disadvantages?*

Pretend your group has been handed a magic wand with a tag that reads, "This wand may be used only once to make a change that will make the world a better place in which to live." What will you do with the wand?

READ-ALOUD
Peavy, Linda, and Ursula Smith. WOMEN WHO CHANGED THINGS.

W_{hy} *do you suppose some people have noticeable handicaps?*

HINT: These are tough questions that most children have already wondered about, but some children may need help in grasping the idea of a handicap that doesn't show. Sharing "Read-Alouds" will be particularly helpful here; these are all sensitive books about people with differences.

FOLLOW-UP QUESTIONS: *Can you think of any kinds of handicaps that don't show? Is it fair that people have handicaps? What does "fair" mean? Why do unfair things happen? Would it be possible to have a world where nothing unfair ever happened?*

READ-ALOUD

Bunting, Eve. FLY AWAY HOME. (homelessness)

Clifton, Lucille. MY FRIEND JACOB. (intellectual disability)

Estes, Eleanor. THE HUNDRED DRESSES. (poverty)

Hanson, Figne. WHAT IF YOU COULDN'T . . . ? A BOOK ABOUT SPECIAL NEEDS.

Konigsburg, E. L. FROM THE MIXED-UP FILES OF MRS. BASIL E. FRANKWEILER. (could intellectual giftedness possibly be considered a handicap?)

McLachian, Patricia. THROUGH GRANDPA'S EYES. (blindness)

Martin, Bill. KNOTS ON A COUNTING ROPE. (blindness, minority)

Yashima, Taro. CROW BOY. (minority)

If you were asked to invent a new holiday, what would it be for? What would you call it? When and how would it be celebrated?

When this question was included on the application form of an Ivy League college, one aspiring student allowed as how she would declare a "procrastinators' day" because she was having so much trouble getting the application written.

What *do you think kitchen utensils would look like if people didn't have thumbs?*

FOLLOW-UP QUESTIONS: *What about tools? What other changes might we have to make in the way we do things?*

READ-ALOUD

Macaulay, David. THE WAY THINGS WORK.

Imagine a world in which video tapes had been invented before the printing press. How might your household, school, or office be different?

FOLLOW-UP QUESTIONS: *If video tapes had been invented first, would print ever have developed? Might we use video and/or print for different purposes than we now do?*

If you had the choice of becoming smarter than you are, would you do it? How might your life be different?

FOLLOW-UP QUESTIONS: *If you were on the committee that had to decide what "super-smart" means, what would you say? What would happen if scientists discovered a way to make everyone who wanted to be super-smart?*

READ-ALOUD

Fitzgerald, John. THE GREAT BRAIN SERIES.

Sobol, Donald J. ENCYCLOPEDIA BROWN SERIES.

Y*ou have been invited to participate in an experiment with a newly developed time machine. You may choose to go forward or backward in time to any place you wish. Would you go? If so, what year or period would you like to land in? Why?*

FOLLOW-UP QUESTION: *If you knew there was a chance you might never come back, would you still go?*

READ-ALOUD

Bond, Nancy. A STRING IN THE HARP.

Bradbury, Ray. LONG AFTER MIDNIGHT.

Eager, Edward. HALF MAGIC.

L'Engel, Madeleine. A WRINKLE IN TIME.

Park, Ruth. PLAYING BEATTIE BOW.

Tanner, Mary. THE WIZARD CHILDREN OF FINN and THE LOST LEGEND OF FINN.

What if, suddenly, all the people in the country woke up speaking different languages so no one could understand anyone else?

HINT: Remember, the legislators can't talk to each other, either.

FOLLOW-UP QUESTIONS: *What would school be like that day? What is the first step the government should take—and what other measures might be needed?*

What if you could invite anybody from the past, present, or future to take a tour of your school or workplace? Whom would you choose?

FOLLOW-UP QUESTIONS: What do you think he or she would be most interested in? What would surprise him or her the most?

What if money grew on trees and everyone could pick as much as they wanted?

HINT: This question can lead to a discussion of the foundations of commerce: e.g., Why do we have money in the first place? What makes something valuable? Would people work if they could pick all the money they wanted?

READ-ALOUD

Baum, Frank. OZMA OF OZ. (may be hard to find)

Heide, Florence Parry. TREEHORN'S TREASURE.

If you could join any expedition that has ever taken place, which one would you choose?

HINT: Most children know of some expeditions from school or television, but parents may need to talk about their own ideas to prime the pump. If background information is hazy, focus on planning your own.

FOLLOW-UP QUESTIONS: *What if you were commissioned to plan a new expedition? Where would you go and how would you get there?*

READ-ALOUD

Blumberg, Rhoda. COMMANDER PERRY IN THE LAND OF THE SHOGUN.

O'Dell, Scott. STREAMS TO THE RIVER, RIVER TO THE SEA: A NOVEL OF SACAGAWEA.

Pretend you are someone whom you are meeting for the first time. How do you think that person would describe you?

HINT: This question gives more practice in taking an objective (abstract) perspective. If it is too difficult, try using a mirror to help participants describe themselves.

Do you think children should have to go to school? Are there other ways they could learn what they need to know? What do they really need to know?

HINT: These questions may spark a good discussion on what is really worth learning—as well as what is the best way to learn it.

FOLLOW-UP QUESTIONS: *Pretend that a computer chip has been developed that can be installed in the brain of every infant right after he or she is born. The chip contains all the facts (such as multiplication tables, spelling words, historical dates, scientific formulas) that people usually memorize in school. Would we still need schools? If not, what would the kids do all day? (Who knows—this possibility may someday exist!)*

READ-ALOUD

Korczak, Janusz. KING MATT THE FIRST.

McKenzie, Ellen Kinat. STARGONE JOHN.

Snyder, Zilpha Keatley. LIBBY ON WEDNESDAY.

Your group has been offered a chance to be the only survivors of the end of the world. You have one day to pack up before you are flown to an isolated, uninhabited tropical island. The group may take only what will fit in one 5 by 5 by 5-foot box and an animal. Will you go? If so, what will you take?

FOLLOW-UP QUESTION: *How would your decisions differ if the island were off the coast of Alaska?*

READ-ALOUD

In addition to the classic survival tales, Daniel Defoe's *Robinson Crusoe* and *Swiss Family Robinson* by Johann Wyss, you may want to sample the following books, which have powerful appeal for today's youngsters (Since many schools have turned to "literature-based" reading programs, you may find your children have already enjoyed some of these titles.):

Farley, Walter. THE BLACK STALLION.

George, Jean Craighead. MY SIDE OF THE MOUNTAIN and JULIE OF THE WOLVES.

Hill, Kirkpatrick. TOUGHBOY AND SISTER.

O'Dell, Scott. ISLAND OF THE BLUE DOLPHINS.

Speare, Elizabeth. THE SIGN OF THE BEAVER.

Steig, William. ABEL'S ISLAND.

If archaeologists one thousand years from now found only the contents of your bedroom, perfectly preserved, what kinds of conclusions might they draw about our civilization?

HINT: Practice in reflecting on something personal from an objective perspective is a natural means of pulling children into more abstract thinking. Because of its demands on higher-level thinking, however, this activity may be difficult for some children. If necessary, remind them that these folks in the future do not have any background knowledge of what current-day life is like.

FOLLOW-UP QUESTION: *What if they found only the contents of your wastebaskets and trash cans instead?*

READ-ALOUD

Dragonwagon, Crescent. HOME PLACE.

Lauber, Patricia. DINOSAURS WALKED HERE AND OTHER STORIES FOSSILS TELL.

Macaulay, David. MOTEL OF THE MYSTERIES.

How *do you think people decide what is "beautiful"?*

HINT: This fundamental issue of aesthetics is, of course, a far more difficult question that it initially appears to be. You may find yourself trying to define the word; try searching for more general concepts: e.g., Is it possible that someone would think something beautiful that someone else thought ugly? (examples?) Who, if anyone, should decide what is "beautiful"? Can you all think of one thing you agree on that is "beautiful"?

READ-ALOUD
Kay, M. M. ORDINARY PRINCESS.
McKinley, Robin. BEAUTY.

If scientists discovered a method to keep people from ever getting any older, would you vote to let them use it? Why or why not?

HINT: Children can come up with some very interesting analyses of this question. If they raise such issues as, "Would people's faces stay the same or would they look older?" "What would happen to babies who are being born?" you can make your own rules about how you think the discovery should work.

FOLLOW-UP QUESTIONS: *If this change were adopted, what other changes might we have to make in our society? What if you alone were given the choice never to get any older—would you do it?*

READ-ALOUD

Babbitt, Natalie. TUCK EVERLASTING.

Barrie, J. M. PETER PAN.

Miles, Miska. ANNIE AND THE OLD ONE.

Where do you think dreams really come from?

FOLLOW-UP QUESTIONS: *How can you be sure that what you think is a dream is not real? Can you prove that you're not in a dream right now?*

READ-ALOUD

Carroll, Lewis. THROUGH THE LOOKING GLASS.

Langton, Jane. THE FLEDGLING.

Van Allsberg, Chris. JUST A DREAM.

Why *does the world need laws?*

HINT: Another good opportunity to expose children to more abstract reasoning. Concrete thinkers tend to focus on laws that directly affect them (e.g., "You shouldn't steal because Jimmy took my ball.") or on personal "law and order" consequences (e.g., "You shouldn't steal because they might put you in jail."). More abstract thinkers tend to deal with broader concepts (how human law relates to natural law, etc.). While neither type of reponse is right or wrong, it is good for children to tune in on different viewpoints while they freely express their own.

FOLLOW-UP QUESTION: *If you were leader of the world and could have only one law, what would it be?*

Imagine that you just ate an apple. Do you think it was alive when you ate it? How can you tell that something is alive?

P*retend there's a robot standing in the room. What would we have to do to him before we could call him human?*

HINT: See discussion in earlier chapter, page 57, for sample conversation.

READ-ALOUD

Milton, Joyce. HERE COME THE ROBOTS.

Slote, Alfred. MY ROBOT BUDDY.

Yolen, Jane. THE ROBOT AND REBECCA.

If you wanted to help out during an energy shortage by giving up some ways in which you use electricity, which ones (if any) could you give up? Which ones (if any) could you absolutely, positively, not do without?

READ-ALOUD
Morey, Walt. CANYON WINTER.

What if it never got dark?

What would you do if you discovered you had the ability exactly to predict weather?

What would furniture look like if our knees bent the other way?

FOLLOW-UP QUESTIONS: *How about automobiles? Other everyday objects?*

Credit to Roger Von Oech's mind-bumping book, *A Whack on the Side of the Head,* for this question.

Why is your home right for the climate you live in? How might it be different if you lived in a different place (e.g., on the equator, the Arctic Circle, a Midwestern farm, a desert, in New York City)?

Would you like to be famous? If you were famous, how would it change your life?

HINT: Follow-up questions might try to elicit ideas about why people want to be famous. Probe for different reasons, e.g., doing good works, having a great talent, making important discoveries, committing a horrible crime, etc. What does money have to do with fame?

READ-ALOUD

Harris, Mark J. CONFESSIONS OF A PRIME TIME KID.

King-Smith, Dick. ACE: THE VERY IMPORTANT PIG.

Paterson, Katherine. COME SING, JIMMY JO.

LEVEL THREE

Mind-Bogglers

These questions will be enjoyed most by mature middle-schoolers, teens, and adults because they call for a considerable degree of abstract reasoning power. Covering many of the classic questions of philosophy, they are purposely designed to challenge even the most mature thinkers.

Note: Reading aloud together is still a wonderful source of conversation and family closeness, even for older teens. I have included a few titles recommended for older readers, although adult fiction and nonfiction are also appropriate for many of these topics. Whatever you choose, don't stop taking some time to read together!

What differences might you find in consumer products if people had prehensile tails (i.e., able to grab and hold things)?

FOLLOW-UP QUESTION: *Why do you suppose people don't have prehensile tails?*

Pretend you leave your bedroom one morning and close the door. Is your bed still there if no one can see it, touch it, or sense it in any other way? How could you prove it?

HINT: One of philosophy's puzzlers, retold. See conversation on pages 9–60 on this question, which is related to the classic, "If a tree falls in the forest and no one can hear it, is there a sound?"

FOLLOW-UP QUESTIONS: *Would there be such a thing as "red" if nothing on the earth had that color? Or does "redness" depend on having red things around?*

Are people just naturally competitive, or is this quality determined by the way they are raised?

FOLLOW-UP QUESTIONS: *What makes people behave competitively? Are you competitive? If so, under what circumstances? If not, why do you think you're not?*

MORE FOLLOW-UP QUESTIONS: *If no one had a spirit of competition, what would society be like? Would there be some way to make people uncompetitive? Would this situation be a desirable one?*

READ-ALOUD

Brooks, Bruce. THE MOVES MAKE THE MAN.

Crutcher, Chris. STOTAN!

Why do you suppose people sing?

FOLLOW-UP QUESTIONS: *Would we be able to communicate m or less effectively if people all sang instead of talking? What wo we do for entertainment? Would people express different types meaning (e.g., be more emotional)? What if you weren't a g singer?*

READ-ALOUD

This one is only tangentially related, but makes interest reading.

Sanders, Scott R. HEAR THE WIND BLOW: AMERICAN FOLK SON RETOLD.

O*nce upon a time people believed that the world was flat and that sea monsters would devour anyone who accidentally slid off the edge. They also believed that night air caused disease, and that taking out a lot of people's blood when they were sick would help them get well. What do you suppose we now believe that people in the future will think sounds really silly?*

HINT: Walter Isaacson's *Pro and Con, Both Sides of Unsettled and Unsettling Arguments* may supplement many of the questions in this section.

Do you think plants can communicate? How?

HINT: If your group doesn't come up with this thought, you might want to add it: Plants grow in response to light and moisture. Is this communication?

If you were asked to create a new season of the year, when would it happen? What would it be like? What would you call it?

READ-ALOUD

Burns, Marilyn. THE REASONS FOR SEASONS.

Jaffrey, Madhur. SEASONS OF SPLENDOR.

How might the course of human civilization have been different if people did not need to eat but could absorb all the nourishment they needed from air and water?

Pretend you leave your bedroom one morning and close the door. Is your bed still there if no one can see it, touch it, or sense it in any other way? How could you prove it?

HINT: One of philosophy's puzzlers, retold. See conversation on pages 9–60 on this question, which is related to the classic, "If a tree falls in the forest and no one can hear it, is there a sound?"

FOLLOW-UP QUESTIONS: *Would there be such a thing as "red" if nothing on the earth had that color? Or does "redness" depend on having red things around?*

A*re people just naturally competitive, or is this quality determined by the way they are raised?*

FOLLOW-UP QUESTIONS: *What makes people behave competitively? Are you competitive? If so, under what circumstances? If not, why do you think you're not?*

MORE FOLLOW-UP QUESTIONS: *If no one had a spirit of competition, what would society be like? Would there be some way to make people uncompetitive? Would this situation be a desirable one?*

READ-ALOUD

Brooks, Bruce. THE MOVES MAKE THE MAN.

Crutcher, Chris. STOTAN!

Why do you suppose people sing?

FOLLOW-UP QUESTIONS: *Would we be able to communicate more or less effectively if people all sang instead of talking? What would we do for entertainment? Would people express different types of meaning (e.g., be more emotional)? What if you weren't a good singer?*

READ-ALOUD

This one is only tangentially related, but makes interesting reading.

Sanders, Scott R. HEAR THE WIND BLOW: AMERICAN FOLK SONGS RETOLD.

W*hat differences might you find in consumer products if people had prehensile tails (i.e., able to grab and hold things)?*

FOLLOW-UP QUESTION: *Why do you suppose people don't have prehensile tails?*

Once upon a time people believed that the world was flat and that sea monsters would devour anyone who accidentally slid off the edge. They also believed that night air caused disease, and that taking out a lot of people's blood when they were sick would help them get well. What do you suppose we now believe that people in the future will think sounds really silly?

HINT: Walter Isaacson's *Pro and Con, Both Sides of Unsettled and Unsettling Arguments* may supplement many of the questions in this section.

Do you think plants can communicate? How?

HINT: If your group doesn't come up with this thought, you might want to add it: Plants grow in response to light and moisture. Is this communication?

You *have been given the opportunity to redesign any appliance or other convenience of modern life. Which one(s) would you work on—and what changes would you make?*

HINT: For redesigning suggestions, try, for example, stove, refrigerator, dishwasher, hair dryer, toaster, television, VCR, automobile, bicycle, airplane, etc.

FOLLOW-UP QUESTION: *Can you think of any new inventions that might be useful?*

READ-ALOUD

Carey, Steven. STEVEN CAREY'S INVENTION BOOK.

Hayden, Robert. EIGHT BLACK AMERICAN INVENTORS.

Yep, Lawrence. DRAGONWINGS.

What if you were asked to write a recipe for success? What ingredients would you put in? Which one is the most important?

HINT: You may find some interesting differences in people's ideas of "success."

Your group has been awarded a contract to redesign the human body for life in the twenty-first century. What changes, if any, will you make? Why?

HINT: To spark thinking about this question you may want to initiate a discussion of how life may be different in the next century from the way it is now.

I*s it possible to think without words?*

Scientists have yet to come up with a final answer to this problem. Try it yourself.

If you could rewind your life up until now like a video film, what would you like to change? Do you think you have choices in the way your personal film will turn out— or was the script written before you were born?

What kind of world—if any—would be possible if there were no such thing as "round"?

HINT: The idea here is that roundness itself—not the word for it—does not exist and cannot be developed (i.e., you can't carve a stone into a round shape and thus discover the wheel).

FOLLOW-UP QUESTION: *Do you suppose there are shapes that might exist on earth but don't?*

How is a football game like the United States Government?

HINT: Trying to find similarities and differences between two unlike concepts is a time-tested mind-expander. Perhaps you can think of other such unlikely comparisons: e.g., How is school like a forest? How is a shopping mall like a zoo? (Or is that one too obvious?) Intelligence researcher Robert Sternberg poses a wonderful problem: "How are the rules for soccer like the rules for math?"

M_{any} societies have traditional "rites of passage" through which adolescents are prepared for and inducted into life in the adult community. What rites of passage are found in your community? Do you think they are beneficial to the young people or to the community? Why or why not?

HINT: "Rites of Passage" may be interpreted to mean anything from a formalized ritual (e.g., Bar or Bat Mitzvah, solo wilderness expedition) to more informal procedures (dating customs, teenaged gangs, driver's license test, etc.).

READ-ALOUD

Because this topic is inherently interesting to teens, there are many fine "coming of age" novels for maturing readers. A sampling:

Desai, Anita. THE VILLAGE BY THE SEA.

Hinton, S. E. THE OUTSIDERS.

Krumgold, Joseph. . . . AND NOW, MIGUEL.

Paulsen, Gary. DOGSONG.

Peck, Robert N. A DAY NO PIGS WOULD DIE.

Rawls, Wilson. WHERE THE RED FERN GROWS.

How much of someone's house would you have to change before it became a different house?

HINT: What if you changed the shape by adding or taking off rooms? What if only one tile in the roof were left? At what point, if ever, is it no longer the same house?

READ-ALOUD

Baum, Frank. OZMA OF OZ. (may be hard to find)

Have you ever wondered if, when you see "green," you are seeing the same "green" as other people are? How might you find out?

$\mathbf{W}hat$ *would the world be like if we suddenly lost all ways of keeping time—and couldn't get them back or invent any new ones?*

HINT: The purpose of this question is to try to imagine a world without the concept of time, not to reinvent sundials, etc. If this proves too difficult, however, it is also interesting for children to try to re-create some system of timekeeping based on what they observe in the natural world.

FOLLOW-UP QUESTIONS: *How would your life be changed? What effect would it have on your home, school, office, community?*

READ-ALOUD

Jones, Deana Wynn. A TALE OF TIME CITY.

Juster, Norton. THE PHANTOM TOLLBOOTH.

Which could we most easily do without: a written alphabet or a system of counting? Why?

HINT: Again, the idea here is not only that these symbol systems do not exist, but also that they can't be invented. This question is super-difficult but fun (and frustrating) to explore.

READ-ALOUD
Juster, Norton. THE PHANTOM TOLLBOOTH.

"It is not possible to step in the same river twice." Do you agree or disagree? Why? Does this quotation have any meaning for life beyond stepping in a river?

FOLLOW-UP QUESTION: *Are you the same person today that you were yesterday?*

How would people live on earth if there were no such thing as fire—or would they?

READ-ALOUD
Heslewood, Juliet. EARTH, AIR, FIRE AND WATER.

In what ways are humans more free than plants? In what ways are they less free?

HINT: Are humans rooted in any way? What limitations—either natural or cultural—do humans have that plants don't have?

Do you think it is possible for something that is against the law to be morally right?

HINT: Finding concrete examples from your own experience makes a question like this more manageable, but sometimes the relationship between moral truth and legal justice is difficult to untangle. A classic dilemma related to this question was posed by Dr. Lawrence Kohlberg in his studies of moral development: A man's wife is dying. There is one drug that can save her, but the druggist refuses to sell it at a price the man can afford. Should the man break the law and steal the drug to save his wife?

READ-ALOUD
Greene, Bette. SUMMER OF MY GERMAN SOLDIER.
White, Robb. DEATHWATCH.

Is thinking about something (e.g., love, a special kind of food, a foreign country) the same as knowing about it? If not, how can you tell the difference?

HINT: Making young people more aware of their internal mental processes makes them better students and thinkers. Personal examples help: When could you think without knowing—or vice versa? What part does mental imagery—making a picture in your mind—play? When do you use it? How?

Have you ever done something good for someone without expecting anything at all in return? Do you think people are ever genuinely unselfish or are they nice, generous, or helpful simply because it makes them feel good?

READ-ALOUD
Sutcliff, Rosemarie. THE SHINING COMPANY.

Some day scientists may develop the ability to produce a perfect clone (copy) of each person, remove the brain, and keep the body in cold storage so that extra parts would be available if needed. For example, if you developed heart, liver, or kidney problems, you could have another copy of your own organ installed. If this happened, would you vote to allow the procedure? Why or why not? Would you order a copy made of yourself?

When is (was) the beginning of time?

HINT: Scientists and philosophers debate whether time—and space, as well—existed before the world began. Do you suppose it is possible to have time without events happening? How about space without anything in it? If there were no time and space before the world began, does this mean that space and time are simply properties of events and objects and not real things themselves? If you find these questions real mind-bogglers, you're in good company!

READ-ALOUD

Lauber, Patricia. SEEING EARTH FROM SPACE.

Merriam, Eve. "LANDSCAPE." (poem) In *Knock at a Star* by X. J. and Dorothy M. Kennedy.

Some people believe that our minds and brains are exactly the same thing. Others argue that the mind is different from the brain. What do you think? Why?

FOLLOW-UP QUESTIONS: *The Greeks believed that thought came from the midriff—where does it come from? Can you measure your thoughts? If injury to the brain can change mental state, what does that mean in terms of this question? What does the "soul" have to do with it?*

Is it OK for people to punish other people? Why or why not?

FOLLOW-UP QUESTION: *What is the real reason for punishment?*

Imagine that you are the president of a university known for its efforts in support of ecology. A man enters your office and offers to donate a million dollars to your school to continue this work. The prospective donor, however, is a notorious scoundrel who has made a fortune from a business that knowingly pollutes the environment. Would you accept the money? What might be the long-range consequences of your decision?

FOLLOW-UP QUESTION: *Should charitable organizations accept money from known criminals?*

What is the ultimate reason for not telling lies?

How long is "now"?

BIBLIOGRAPHY

CREATIVE THINKING AND QUESTIONING

Costa, Arthur, and Lawrence Lowery. *Techniques for Teaching Thinking*. Pacific Grove, Calif.: Midwest Publications, 1989.

deBono, Edward. *deBono's Thinking Course*. New York: Facts on File, 1985.

Dillon, J. T. *Questioning and Teaching*. New York: Teachers College Press, 1988.

Ewing, A. C. *The Fundamental Questions of Philosophy*. London: Routledge & Kegan Paul, 1985.

Lipman, Matthew. *Philosophy Goes to School*. Philadelphia: Temple University Press, 1988.

Matthews, Gareth B. *Dialogues with Children*. Cambridge, Mass.: Harvard University Press, 1984.

———. *Philosophy and the Young Child*. Cambridge, Mass.: Harvard University Press, 1980.

Sternberg, Robert, and Richard Wagner, eds. *Practical Intelligence*. Cambridge: Cambridge University Press, 1986.

Stock, Gregory. *The Book of Questions*. New York: Workman Publishing Co., 1987.

———. *The Kids' Book of Questions*. New York: Workman Publishing Co., 1988.

Von Oech, Roger. *A Whack on the Side of the Head*. New York: Warner Books, 1973.

GUIDES TO READ-ALOUDS

Gillespie, J., and C. Gilbert. *Best Books for Children*. New York: R. R. Bowker Company, 1985.

Hearne, Betsy. *Choosing Books for Children*. New York: Delacorte Press, 1981.

Landsberg, Michele. *Reading for the Love of It*. New York: Prentice Hall, 1987.

Lipson, Eden Ross. *The New York Times Parent's Guide to the Best Books for Children*. New York: Times Books, 1988.

Oppenheim, J., B. Brenner, and B. D. Boegehold. *Choosing Books for Kids*. New York: Ballantine Books, 1986.

Rudman, Marsha Kabakow. *Children's Literature: An Issues Approach*. New York: Longman & Co., 1976.

Trelease, Jim. *The New Read-Aloud Handbook*. New York: Penguin Books, 1989.

COMMUNICATING WITH CHILDREN

Faber, Adele, and Elaine Mazlish. *How to Talk So Kids Will Listen and Listen So Kids Will Talk*. New York: Avon Books, 1980.

——. *Siblings Without Rivalry*. New York: Avon Books, 1988.

Ginott, Haim G. *Between Parent and Child*. New York: Avon Books, 1969.

Weiner, Harvey S. *Talk with Your Child*. New York: Viking Penguin, 1988.

UNDERSTANDING AND HELPING CHILDREN WITH EXPRESSIVE LANGUAGE PROBLEMS

McCabe, Allyssa. *Language Games to Play with Your Child*. New York: Fawcett Columbine, 1987.

Vail, Priscilla. *Clear and Lively Writing*. New York: Walker & Co., 1981.

——. *Smart Kids with School Problems*. New York: NAL, 1989.